GLOBAL HEALING

Poverty, Migration and Refugees, Race and Religion, War, Morality.

Robin Arthur

En Route Books and Media, LLC
Saint Louis, MO, USA

⊕ENROUTE
Make the time

En Route Books and Media, LLC
5705 Rhodes Avenue
St. Louis, MO 63109

Cover Design: Aaron Arthur. The cover depicts Four Horsemen of the Apocalypse, an 1887 painting by Viktor Vasnetsov and represents Death, Famine, War and Conquest. The author passed away in 1926, so this work is in the public domain in its country of origin and other countries and areas where the copyright term is the author's life plus 95 years or fewer.

Hon. Editors: Stephen Cunningham and Aaron Arthur

ISBN: 978-1-956715-55-2
Library of Congress Control Number: 2022939230

Wars in history have been fought for either the cause of nationhood or the cause of one's religion, both of which are accidents of birth.

CONTENTS

INTRODUCTION

I am not about to throw caution to the wind. But what I see blowing in it may be a sliver of hope. Covid–19, the monster which put the brakes on world progress, consumed some 6.7 million people, spared neither princes nor paupers, and dragged millions into poverty, is now about to enter the domain of history.

If I were to illustrate this mood of expectation, I would probably paint an image of the Ark atop a hill loaded with expectant hearts on board as they watch Noah open the window of his wooden craft to free a bird into the skies who would bring back tidings of the abatement of that great flood.

The world is on a cusp of change. Covid-19 may be on the way out, but it's leaving behind a trail of tribulation that can perhaps be analogized with the aftermath of a war.

In a news report released on 17 January 2022, the International Labour Organization (ILO) said it had downgraded its forecast for labour market recovery in 2022, projecting a deficit in hours worked globally equivalent to 52 million jobs. Global unemployment is expected to remain above pre-Covid-19 levels until at least 2023. This year it is estimated to be at 207 million, compared to 186 million in 2019.[1]

But this book is not going to dwell on how the world is going to confront this challenge. Let's leave the unravelling of these knots to the wisdom and intellect of economists, market analysts and industrialists.

Instead, this work seeks to present five conundrums that a changing world will confront increasingly in the future, namely: poverty, migration and refugees, race and religion, the threat of war and national morality.

The irony of it all is that while we can now split the atom, design artificial intelligence to replicate human behaviour, make excursions into space and even speak with hubris about science's pursuit to put an end to death, we have not yet grasped the secret of making peace with one another. We turn to weapons to do the contrary and strut around feigning to belong to an elitist civilisation. Switch on your television screens and you see it all there.

What you see is war, conflict and strife, desperate poverty, hate driven tragedies and amoral actions. And what are we doing about it? A little, too late. Instead,

---

[1] World Employment and Social Outlook: Trends 2022. Excerpt taken from the ILO's News Release, 17 January 2022. "Copyright ©International Labour Organization 2022."

we're playing roulette with nuclear buttons. This book examines the challenges that stand in the way of world progress and threaten the decent survival of the human race.

POVERTY

A wind of change may have swept across the world in the last three decades. By the end of the 1980s, the communist ideology was fast losing its appeal across the former Soviet Union, forcing new thinking on a government that finally unleashed Perestroika. The domino effect was felt across East Europe, among former Soviet satellites and in tandem the Berlin Wall fell. As the final Uruguay Round on GATT (General Agreements on Tariffs and Trade) got underway, borders opened for most countries across the world. The political equations changed and world leaders began to talk of a new world order, neglecting the fact that at the time, three fourths of the human race were mired in a mess, driven by poverty, civil strife and hopelessness.

In the last decade, we have seen evidence of a growth in literacy and a simultaneous spike in the development index of developing countries with China and India leading the pack. So, what this says is that the economic profile of the developing world has got a face lift and that the "no poverty" and "zero hunger" goals of the UN's 2030 agenda for sustainable development has had some impact on the campaign against poverty. But the fact that Covid-19 could derail the campaign, tells me that poverty is linked to something deeper than economics.

Globally, the number of people living in extreme poverty had actually declined from 36 percent in 1990 to 10 per cent in 2015. But the pace of change is decelerating, and the Covid-19 crisis risks reversing decades of progress. Now, more than 700 million people have to be dug out of extreme poverty - the majority living on less than $1.90 a day live in sub-Saharan Africa. Worldwide, the poverty rate in rural areas is 17.2 percent.[2]

In a news release, the UN University World Institute for Development Economics Research (UNU-WIDER) has warned that the economic fallout from the global pandemic could increase global poverty by as much as half a billion people, or eight percent of the total human population. This would be the first time

---

[2] United Nations. https://www.un.org/sustainable-development/poverty/

that poverty has increased globally in thirty years, since 1990.[3]

The authors of the UNU-WIDER study say that a setback of this size would reverse a decade of global progress on poverty reduction. This study affirms that the achievement of the UN Sustainable Development Goals on "no poverty" and "zero hunger," is under considerable threat.

It's just as well that the results of the study have galvanized compassion for vulnerable communities around the world. The UNU says in its report that Oxfam has been calling on world leaders to agree on an Emergency Rescue Package of USD 2.5 trillion paid for through the immediate cancellation or postponement of $1 trillion in debt repayments, a $1 trillion increase in IMF Special Drawing Rights, and an additional $500 billion in aid.[4]

I don't want to dampen any optimism, but at the end of the 20th century, developing nations had passed around their hats for development funds, but funding

---

[3] UN University (UNU – WIDER) https://www.wider.unu.edu/publication/estimates-impact-covid-19-global-poverty

[4]   https://unu.edu/media-relations/releases/covid-19-fallout-could-push-half-a-billion-people-into-poverty-in-developing-countries.html

by the World Bank and the IMF probably only made veteran borrowers of these nations at the time.

The erstwhile Colombo Plans, Poverty Summits, Commonwealth conferences and non-aligned movements may have got underway but have not been able to do anything in a significant way to alleviate the developing world's chronic problems with poverty. Neither have the experiments with socialist governance nor capitalist doctrines been able to change the destinies of those people at the margins.

So, what is it that can lift the less developed world from poverty? That is something I examine in this book along with the other socio-political conundrums that challenge our changing world.

There is, I believe, a more sustainable approach to ending poverty in a way that would make the world resilient to future natural disasters which push people back into poverty. Covid-19 has not necessarily, from an economic point of view, devasted high and middle income populations. It has hit the world's poorest in developing countries where the social climate in which economic development can germinate has not yet been prepared. That is something to think about, and that is what I express in this book.

MIGRATION AND REFUGEES

The migration of peoples is as old as the hills. This book, however, examines migration and people's movement driven by economic and political factors and which got a rough start in the early 20th century.

It's very obvious that new challenges to Western societies in our time, including the need for steady growth of their populations and the imperative to compete with world production to boost their economies, have prompted them to look for manpower skills through immigration. It's known that immigration is both an opportunity and a challenge.

In the late 19th and early 20th centuries, North America turned to Britain and Europe for manpower to develop an agrarian economy as well as to build their country's infrastructure. Their governments resisted arrivals of the Chinese, Japanese and East Indians, following protests from white residents. But in the late 20th century the migration pattern was upended.

The current global estimate is that there were around 272 million international migrants in the world in 2019, which equates to 3.5 per cent of the global population. The United States of America has been the main country of destination for international migrants since 1970. Since then, the number of foreign-born people residing in the country has more than quadrupled – from less than 12 million in 1970, to close to 51 million in 2019. Germany, the second top destination for migrants, has also observed an increase over the years, from 8.9 million in 2000 to 13.1 million in 2019. More than 40 per cent of all international migrants worldwide in 2019 (112 million) were born in Asia, primarily originating from India (the largest country of origin), China, and South Asian countries including Bangladesh, Pakistan and Afghanistan.[5]

Global migration and mobility are today at the heart of global change, not only impacting economic and development policy and human capital, but also challenging social and political inclusion, religious diversity and the blind sentiment of nationalism.

RACE AND RELIGION

This narrative has a Canadian perspective. Canada's early history has been stained by stories of prejudiced treaties with the First Nations as well as by those ugly Anglo-French battles and race-driven legislation intro-

---

[5] McAuliffe, M. and B. Khadria, eds., 2019. *World Migration Report 2020*. International Organization for Migration (IOM), Geneva.

duced to bar the entry into Canada of the Japanese, Chinese and East Indian communities. But the nation has made amends.

Now with a Charter that guarantees rights and freedoms to all Canadians, regardless of race or faith, Canada is truly becoming a template for the model state. Its policy makers recognize that immigration is about economics, but they also realize that multiculturalism is a work in progress. There must be a sense of one's common humanity, despite the diversity of cultures. Therefore, in the new milieu, the country's city planners have been brought into the process of creating multicultural cities.

The importance of religion as one aspect of diversity has been recognised, and the need for concomitant research or policy capacity to address many of the issues that arise from religious diversity is being prioritised, as ideological differences may prove more intractable than the racial divide.

A clash of civilizations is inevitable. So, as people of different faiths take up residence in the West – and that will happen because immigration spurs economic growth – the challenge of accommodating religious diversity, especially within the framework of secular governance, gets more pointed.

In Chapter III, I roll out the narrative on how Canada is challenged by religious diversity, especially with calls from Hindu disciples for a waterway to immerse the ashes of the deceased and calls, as well, from Muslims to include the Sharia law in Canada's penal code.

Canada has confronted these challenges excellently. But as the country's pluralism gets deep-seated, the challenge will be greater. I say greater because I believe public opinion surveys reveal that relations between faith communities and secular Canadians are now a very important preoccupation. There is a significant demographic change in the world, characterized by considerable growth in the percentage of Westerners who are not Christian as well as an increase in Westerners reporting no religion. There is already evidence of an exponential growth in religions from South and East Asia, Africa and the Middle East.

The hundreds of thousands of newcomers that are headed to countries in the West every year are not going to leave their religion at the door and come in. That is because culture at its heart is religious.

How, then, does a country accommodate religious diversity and welcome an intellectual workforce of diverse cultures in a secular framework of governance? How do we grow multicultural cities? What is the challenge that social inclusion or exclusion poses? How do we police in a multicultural society? What's the nature of identity politics? How do we deal with racial prejudice? In this book, I cast a light on those and several other conundrums that challenge migrant recipient countries and I present Canada as a model.

So, indeed, Canada recognizes the new challenge that it's up against and that religious diversity is intrinsically part of the package that multiculturalism brings.

In 2011, 2.4 million people identified themselves as either Muslim, Hindu, Sikh or Buddhist, accounting for 7.2 percent of Canada's population. More specifically, slightly over one million individuals identified themselves as Muslim, making up 3.2 percent of the nation's population.[6]

THE THREAT OF WAR

As I'm thinking up an opening line for this narrative, the bullets are flying over Ukraine, and I can hear echoes of Bob Dylan's wail crying out saying "How many times should the cannon balls fly before they're forever banned?"

---

[6] Statistics Canada, *Canada Day...by the numbers*, 2022.

In 1945 when those deadly guns of World War II fell silent, the world stopped to think and collectively said "Never Again". But some memories are short-lived. A couple of years ago, the former American president Donald Trump and his counterpart in North Korea were sabre rattling, flinging threats of a nuclear confrontation. Now analysts observing developments in the Russian-Ukrainian war are also talking about the possible escalation of this war to dangerous thresholds.

The formation of the League of Nations after World War 1 may have been a great start to keeping the peace, providing deterrents to the escalation of conflict, but its limited mandate put a cap on its powers of intervention, so it was dismantled unceremoniously as World War II descended upon us.

The formation of the United Nations was a brave initiative but it's a world body that's also incapacitated by its mandate, which is why there have been calls for UN reform. It has been criticized for being an exclusive nuclear club with five nuclear powers calling the shots. A consequence of that structure is that a veto from any one of the permanent members can halt any possible action the UN Security Council may take.

Its peacekeeping forces were never mandated to deter war; instead, they were mandated to monitor peace after the signing of peace treaties.

NATO has been able to flex its muscle and stop wars, but it's not a world body. It's a big boys club mandated to protect the borders of most European nations and two countries in North America.

So, what are the safeguards that the world body can rustle up today to challenge the inevitability of war and secure the world from that terrible eventuality of a handful of world leaders setting the world on fire?

What are the options? Is a reformed and restructured United Nations going to fortify the world body? Do we need a world army with the muscle to deter and stop a war, intervening when any one of the world's 195 nations is threatened? I don't exactly know. What I do know is that darkness cannot drive away darkness. Light can do that.

In this book, I share some light with two scenarios to open up the conversation. It takes the courage to dream of the day when war will be relegated to the back pages of history and bring about radical change in the way mankind's reason and heart evolves to challenge war with peace.

NATIONAL MORALITY

The reform of the morality of nations can be as challenging as the task of eliminating poverty in the developing world; confronting the new realities of a rapidly emerging migration movement or holding back the destructive instinct for war.

In this chapter, I argue that in almost all cases, citizens of a state have definite traits of national character which bring them together as one people bonded by a set of spiritual beliefs, customs, traditions and linguistic commonality and that it's this commonality of national character that promotes a sense of nationhood. What we have also come to realize in time is that morality is central to the spirit of nations and that a decline in morality ultimately affects the prosperity and peace of nations.

The curious question that this conversation raises, however, is: "What moral decline am I talking about?" I am talking about the dramatic leap forward to rebellion against restraint in the second half of the 20th century, when countries in the West were stumbling out of post-war depression. I am talking about the careless drift to licentiousness and godlessness; the plunge into hedonism, the seeking of gratification from the abuse of alcohol and drugs, promiscuity and violence.

Most young teenagers today are taught to navigate the waters of life through power, wealth and fame. A soccer star might rank first among some of their heroes, and God might just be dismissed as an idea. The perpetuating notion that man is the master of his fate and captain of his soul is scary.

The atheist community has long held the notion that morality is driven by the natural order of human consciousness. It's commonly assumed that people act in ways that are dictated by a moral obligation and that morality commits us to that social consciousness. What this says is that the world can be moral without God. I respond to that notion drawing on a piece of European history which outlines the immorality of the age prior to the Edict of Milan in 313 and the narrative of how Christian societal reform changed the order of the era, kicking out slavery and infanticide from the immoral fabric of nations.

It's no secret that we see a trend to godlessness as well, in a significant section of our society, driven by a notion that the universe created itself some 14 billion years ago. I address this in my book *Science and the God Elusion*, which I released in 2019, and I present a brief riposte to that doctrine in this book.

This chapter carries a brief narrative on the "Big Bang" and the skepticism with which the theory was received by a section of the scientific world. I also present Charles Darwin's admission in the final edition of his book *On The Origin of Species* that life forms were first breathed by the Creator. I suspect that fact is known to merely a few of those who have read his first editions. I also address the questions that finally ended the euphoria over the Miller-Urey experiment in 1953 that sought scientific confirmation that life could have evolved with the serendipity of amino acids joining together in thousands of units to form proteins which could have combined into symbiotic relationships we refer to as life. The eminent scientist Dr. Gerald Schroedder, author of the book *The Hidden Face of God,* referred to that scientific enquiry as "one long study in failure."[7]

The defining question, however, that comes up in this morality discourse is this: How does moral decline affect national life and economic progress? I have given that question a whirl.

---

[7] Schroeder, L. Gerald, *The Hidden Face of God*, Simon & Schuster, p.58.

CHAPTER 1

POVERTY

The International Monetary Fund (IMF), by its classification of economic factors, affirms that there are 152 Less Developed Countries (LDCs) in the world with a current population of around 6.62 billion. That makes up 85.2 percent of the world's population.[1] Their economies show a high proportion of subsistence agriculture with a very limited application of technology. Any manufacturing is minimal.

Their population is characterized by a greater proportion of young people who consume goods but are not productive. Education is not accessible to a significant portion of the masses, and even primary education is neither free nor compulsory. Consequently, the rapid accretion of population has meant rapid numerical growth of the poor, especially because family planning programs have met opposition from religious groups.

Poverty perpetuates and malnutrition is evidenced in scores of LDCs. It's a vicious trap. The population

---

[1] Worlddata.info

control programs have acted just as water would on a duck's back. The rapid growth of the poor has brought an endless flow of unskilled migrants from farms to towns in an unbridled way, translating underemployment in the hinterland to unemployment in the towns, forcing a breakdown of municipal services, worsening conditions in the slums, triggering disease and water shortages, homelessness, crime and prostitution.

A too rapid increase in population in the LDCs has also outpaced capital accumulation, and although some of the countries in the Far East and Asian subcontinent, for example, have been able to raise investment in industry and jump start largely stagnant gross domestic product growth in the last decade, their record with raising living standards across the board has been unimpressive.

India appears to have made moderate economic progress at the turn of the century, but in tandem we also saw evidence of a spike in literacy levels. According to the United Nations Development Program (UNDP) administrator Achim Steiner, India lifted 271 million people out of extreme poverty in a 10-year time period from 2005 to 2016.

Here's an illustration of the concomitance of literacy and poverty. It demonstrates how with a spike in literacy, poverty levels in India had dropped between 1961 and 2019.

In 1961, India's literacy rate hovered at around 40.4 percent according to the Census of India report. At about the same time, Dandekar and Rath, on behalf of the Indian government, estimated that the poverty rate in the 1960s remained generally constant at 41 percent.[2] Notice their concomitance? Then almost six decades later, the National Statistical Commission survey affirmed that India's literacy rate rose to 77.7 percent in 2018[3] when around the same period, the United Nations Millennium Development Goals (MDG) programme was reporting that India's poverty rate had dropped significantly to 6.7 percent of the country's population.[4] Literacy and poverty are concomitant. Literacy levels rise, the poverty rate falls.

Poverty in Africa is chronic for several reasons. But as this book argues, the root of all poverty lies outside the bounds of economic theory. The classical Keynes

---

[2] Dandekar and Rath: "Poverty in India" Economic and Political Weekly, 6 (2) 9 January 1971. Retrieved 16 August 2017.

[3] National Statistical Commission, NSO 2018, P.1.

[4] Puja Mehra, 2 April 2016, "8% GDP growth helped reduce poverty"- UN report, The Hindu. Retrieved 16 August 2017.

GDP expansion approach to economic development assumes a human development index (HDI) factor that is grossly higher than subsistence living. The point being made is that there can be little GDP expansion unless the social and cultural climate in which economic development can germinate is first prepared.

Geographers point out that the roots of Africa's food crisis are manifold: climate change, deforestation and soil erosion and consequently poor agriculture. But Africa's real problems which perpetuate its misery are firstly population pressure and, of course, warfare. Famines and food shortages are often regarded as a product of drought. But even in the absence of drought, Africa has experienced hunger. So, drought does not always translate into disaster and as often assumed, the problem is not a lack of agricultural productivity or difficult climatic conditions. Sub-Saharan Africa has millions of hectares of fertile soil. The African continent could feed itself.

It may be well to consider that the rate of population accretion has a more fundamental link with food shortage, because it continues to drain land resources. The famine of the mid-1980s that drove millions of Ethiopians in search of food and water may have been triggered by drought. But seen from an academic lens, the consistent two percent drop in food production per year and three percent growth in population since the 1960s, reflects Africa's real problems with feeding itself. Take Ethiopia for example: In 1950 its total population was down at 18.4 million which later bumped up to 109.2 million in 2018.[5]

In comments over population growth, in the ongoing pages, I argue that population accretion has everything to do with the literacy levels of a nation's citizenry and that poverty cannot be rooted out, without achieving an equivalency in the growth rates of population and food production—the Malthusian doctrine that has weathered the test of time. How do you do that? I believe you can achieve that balance by creating the social and cultural climate in which literacy and, consequently, economic development can mushroom.

Although on the surface, poverty may appear to be at the heart of all those conundrums that lower the Human Development Index (HDI) in less developed countries—whether those be critical mass migration, food shortages or the unproductive toil ratio - I think that at the heart of this malaise is something more

---

[5] "World Population Prospects" United Nations Department of Economic and Social Affairs, Population Division. Retrieved November 9, 2019. https://en.wikipedia.org/wiki/Demographics_ of_Ethiopia#Population

fundamental. That something fundamental is literacy. Think of poverty and population accretion as a product of alarmingly low literacy and not as the problem itself.

It can be argued quite simply with an illustration that demonstrates how countries that have put education on top of national priorities have emerged as economic giants while other nations in this grouping have not. Let's examine some of those illustrations.

THE JAPANESE MIRACLE

Japan's resurrection from the ashes of World War II and its post-war emergence as an economic juggernaut is often referred to as the Japanese miracle—a mystifying feat that stunned the world's economists. So, what was the mystifying genie that enabled Japan to overtake the developed world after a demoralizing defeat that deflated their erstwhile pride in national superiority?

A slew of case studies credit the country's trans- formation to the US-led Allied occupation of Japan whose policy makers introduced change aimed at democratising Japanese institutions and the political system, resting sovereignty with the people, granting the emperor the mere status of a state figurehead, introducing equal rights for women, strengthening grassroots political participation and abolishing military supremacy.

But the US-led Allied occupation of Japan ended in 1952, and Japan came into its own then and began a reform process strategizing the two paths to national supremacy—firstly, one that would create large conglomerates through amalgamation to bring about synthesis and synergy of the manufacturing, finance and trading groups linked through mutual ownership of stock and second, the commitment to develop widespread education for the creation of a well-educated workforce that would be foundational to the country's technological advancement.

The Japanese prioritised a reform process of its education sector framing policies designed to reflect the culture and aspirations of its people. A course in moral education was reinstated, despite fears it would lead to a renewal of heightened nationalism. The education system was reformed to reflect its age-old culture and philosophical ideas that uphold the noble view that moral and character development must be integral to education. Likewise, there was strong indoctrination in national ambitions and in the conviction that education was to play a key role in Japan's remarkable economic resurgence.

Now Japan's impressive literacy rate at 99 percent[6] is credited to be the key to its emergence as an economic juggernaut. It ranks third in the world economy after the US and China with a nominal GDP of $5.06 trillion.[7]

THE FOUR ASIAN TIGERS

Despite the fact that Africa is more resource rich than many other regions of the world, not one of its states can boast the economic miracle that countries in South East Asia have made happen.

During the 1970s, at a time when much of the developed world was reeling under recession and low commodity prices brought a decline in living standards, the four Asian nations, namely South Korea, Taiwan, Hong Kong and Singapore bumped up their economies with rapid export-led industrialization. Low labour costs, stable political regimes and an open mind to foreign investments smoothened the pace. But what must be realized is that at the heart of this engine driving economic growth in South East Asia was a rapidly

---

[6] Organization for Economic Cooperation and Development (OECD) PISA.

[7] World Bank.

growing literate society. The "four tigers" as these nations were labeled, currently have a literacy rate that is well above 95 percent, and Indonesia, the Philippines and Malaysia are fast edging up to that rung in the literacy ladder.

THE CHINESE EXPERIMENT

Although the Western-born economist has responded with some scepticism to the socialist doctrine of collective agricultural production for the common good, China's People's Commune, which has brought about organization that has little rival elsewhere in the developing world, is hailed as a great success story by the American economist, the late John Kenneth Galbraith, in his book *A China Passage*.

The Chinese People's Commune was the highest of three administrative tiers in the rural belts of the country from the late fifties to the early eighties, until modernisation of the economy prompted a transition to townships. These communes began as an amalgamation of collective farms but grew to become administrative tiers managing economic and social activity within government purview.

During China's Great Leap Forward, the Chinese people forfeited private plots to common ownership, and wages were egalitarian in consonance with the socialist doctrine. The common good, national aspirations, the commitment to work hard and participation in economic development at the grass-roots level were the cornerstones of the ideology driving economic activity in the communes.

This can occur only in an environment where literacy levels are peaking. In his book *Factors in Economic Development*, Professor Cairncross affirms that development is not governed in any country by economic factors alone. Development in the Third World is dependent on several non-economic factors among which are social attitudes, political conditions and human endowments. "The key to development," the professor notes, "lies in the minds of men, in the institutions in which their thinking finds expression and in the play of opportunity on ideas and institutions."[8]

He contends that an underdeveloped economy is not only required to raise the levels of investment in order to initiate growth, but it is also required to transform the social, religious and political institutions which act as obstacles to economic progress. "Conse-

---

[8] *Factors in Economic Development*, A.K Cairncross, Copyright 2011, Ist Edition, published by Routledge, republished by permission of Taylor & Francis Group.

quently, economic development cannot take place unless men are educated."

China's adult literacy rate in 2018 was at the top of the ladder's rung at 99.8 percent. With rising literacy levels, its poverty rate fell from an appalling 88 percent in 1981 to 0.7 percent in 2015, as measured by the percentage of people living on the equivalent of US $1.90 or less per day.[9] It now takes second place among the world's biggest economies with a gross domestic product (GDP) of USD 14.72 trillion, second only to the United States of America.[10]

CAPITALISM: ONE SIZE CAN'T FIT ALL

The failure of socialist governance across some parts of the developing world appears to mistakenly confirm that the only realistic path to economic growth is capitalist production. This observation does not seek to find fault with capitalism as an engine of production. Indeed, the criticism, hitherto, has tended to dwell on the cultural and moral disapproval of some features of the capitalist system. But capitalism has, unequivocally, created the highest standards of living ever known on

---

[9] "Overview," Worldbank.org.
[10] World Bank.

earth. The erstwhile contrast between West Berlin and East Berlin was most convincing. Indeed, capitalism did also wipe out slavery and serfdom in the developed world of the 19th century. In America, the industrial, capitalist North wiped out an agrarian and feudal culture that promoted slavery in the South.

But notwithstanding such historical evidence, it may be erroneous to conceive of capitalism as a money-spinner mantra. There is something very fundamental to grapple with, in any approach to political economy and to the evaluation of several social systems. The seed in which capitalism can germinate must first be prepared. Since economic systems are about men or of state raising capital for men, the search for political economies should begin with identifying man's most essential characteristics in the context of his development. The search leads one to conclude, as capitalists have, that man's mind, the rational faculty, is his basic means of survival.

Precisely because the capitalist seed germinates best in the entrepreneurial, and by inference, an intellectual society, progress can come out of individual surplus, from the energy, the creative overabundance of those men whose ability produces more than their personal consumption requires, or those who are intellectually and financially able to seek out the new, think outside the box and challenge change.

The factors defining the capitalism doctrine bear the unmistakable stamp of the entrepreneur's mind. Its conformance to capital utilitarianism, its achievements in the field of science and technology, its adventuristic temper may all be traced to the spirit of rationalization, and this straightaway should lead anyone to deduce that capitalism can have no place in the developing world, until the social and cultural climate is ready for it.

This is the stark truth that LDC governments have to grapple with when planning economic development. Education is at the heart of economic development and only when this is fully realized, can there be a reversal in the approach to development in the developing world.

At the end of the last century, governments of Less Developed Countries were spending 20 percent on defence and less than three percent on education. That reflected a priority perspective that was out of touch with reality. So, it seems reasonable to assume that the society which invests more in people would advance more rapidly and inherit the future and that there will be no universal recipe for development in societies where the rational faculty is not trained to go forward.

It is perhaps a foregone conclusion that the econo-mies of the developing world cannot be analyzed in the light of classical theories and planned in terms of the conceptual apparatus of a Keynes or a Leontief. Far too much lies outside the organized sector and hence this never-ending search for a growth model applicable to poverty-stricken conditions in the developing world.

A poor country can aspire to be a rich country through industrialization only where factors, other than economic, provide the social and cultural climate in which literacy can thrive. Civil strife, the refugee problem, repression by state authority, dictatorships, low life expectancy, critical mass migration and the appalling quality of life in the developing world, all point to the need for a fundamental precondition of development, which is a mature and ubiquitous climate of literacy.

KEY TO DEVELOPMENT

The conclusion too often drawn is that a poor country can only become a rich country by concentrating all its resources on industrialization. But what is not realized, perhaps, is that if economic development through industrialization has failed to deliver across the developing world, it is because capital formation, though necessary, is not a sufficient condition for economic development.

In the developing world, India provides a classic example. It's experiment with capital as the engine of production has transformed its middle class into a massive consumer group of about 700 million people. But it has failed to pull its poor out of misery in the rural regions. "India lives in its villages" wrote the country's first Prime Minister, Jawaharlal Nehru, in his book *A Discovery of India*.

The key to development is dependent on several non-economic factors that hinder economic progress, among which are quaint social beliefs, communal passion, religious heterogeneity, political conditions, but most of all, an appallingly high rate of illiteracy in the rural regions.

If the campaign to boost literacy in less developed countries can transform the world's marginalized societies into a powerhouse of human capital, we will have driven poverty into the pages of history.

THE BEST PRACTICES INITIATIVE

In a conversation, some years ago, with Dr. Wally N'Dow, former Secretary General of the United Nations Centre for Human Settlements (UNCHS), we spoke about the concomitance of poverty and literacy and he said to me: "The job cannot be done by cursing the darkness. We need a new approach, a creative and constructive effort that can only come if we forge a global partnership between national governments and local communities, between the public and private sectors."

Dr. N'Dow was in Dubai at the time for the Dubai International Conference – a countdown to Habitat II which got underway in Istanbul where UNCHS celebrated the launching of the Best Practices initiative, analyzing and cataloguing the best urban practices in the world.

He said to me: "No one should any longer ignore the fact that man must share a common responsibility for a common future." The initial selection of Best Practices highlighted programs that have achieved the most tangible improvements in the lives and livelihoods of women, men and children, the cities and communities that are able to form lasting partnerships between local and national governments and community organizations.

The initiatives have resulted in changes in legislation, policies and decision-making, ensuring that the benefits to people are sustainable and sustained. A UNCHS report at the time had affirmed that the Best Practices that had emerged may have gone miles in the endeavour of making life more sustainable for the future. Chattanooga in Tennessee, for example, had experimented with sustainable community development with the vision of becoming "an environmental city," just as Leicester in the United Kingdom, Gotenburg in Sweden, Tilburg in the Netherlands or Hamilton-Wentworth in Canada.

In an early morning meeting with Dr. N'Dow, I provoked the question about how urban development in developing countries could ever forge ahead if the Best Practices that have evolved so far have not focused on literacy's role in human development. The point being made was that migration to urban centers, accretion of population, widespread unemployment and the perpetuation of poverty – all of which culminate in the breakdown of municipal services in the towns and generate violence and social unrest – are part of a cycle that is born out of low literacy levels in the developing world.

Dr. N'Dow had conceded that education was going to be an issue Habitat II would address because human resource is at the heart of economic development. "Indeed, there is need for advocacy on our part to underline literacy's role in economic development and social progress," he told me. "I do believe, just as you say, that it is at the foundation of most of the challenges we face and therefore literacy should be at the foundation of all our effort."

If mankind is going to share a common future, it's going to take a global society to put an end to poverty with a campaign of literacy that will light the path ahead.

The 9-nation Education For All summit in Delhi in 1993 was the first ever initiative by the world community to put the spotlight on education and identify it as key to solving the problems in the developing world. Bangladesh, Brazil, China Egypt, India, Indonesia, Mexico, Nigeria and Pakistan together, at the time, accounted for half the world's population, but they also accounted for 70 percent of the world's 905 million illiterates according to a UN document on education. Sadly, but not unexpectedly, the summit was downsized in importance even before it started. Although the summit was hailed as a milestone in the literacy crusade, that initiative was a non-starter. The cost of reaching the goal of basic education for all nine nations was estimated to be about $5 billion, or the approximate cost of 25 Boeing 777s at the time. That's loose change for our billionaires.

Earlier in the 1960s, the UN appealed to rich nations to apportion one percent of national incomes to development of poor nations. Sadly, aid was, instead, diverted to projects such as power stations, irrigation schemes, railways and factories which would create future wealth as capitalist states had then envisioned. But as history records it, the gulf between the rich and poor widened in the 1970s. The question about what must be prioritised in the development process is not a chicken or egg question: social change must prepare the path ahead to fire up prosperity.

The United Nations must be pressed to take up the mantle, forge the pathway ahead and invite our big banks, our multinational corporations, our billionaires and NGOs to come together and ignite this dream. It's a shared future after all. Think of what can result from a literate powerhouse. Think also of what can result from a status quo.

Dr. N'Dow, before departing from Dubai said to me: "Of the 100 babies being born every day, at least 80 are from the LDCs. If we do not give these children the skills, the ABCs to empower themselves, the burden of life will ultimately impact on all of humanity."

The process, which will ultimately produce the climate in which the seeds of economic development can bloom, may unfold over the next ten years. But in the life of Less Developed Nations that have for long bitten the dust, a decade is like an evening gone.

Education is the catalyst to ending poverty.

CHAPTER II

MIGRATION AND REFUGEES

It's been said in so many splendid ways. The writer V.S. Naipaul who moved from Trinidad to rural England, spoke of the transition as the "enigma of arrival." Nino Ricci, a Canadian novelist, whose parents came to Canada leaving their home in northern Italy, and who tells his story in my book *Canada's Immigrants, Heroes and Countrymen*, says that without a point of departure there can be no arrival.

Ricci says that when he was writing his first novel, he was somewhat surprised to find himself going back for his material to that very first visit to his parents' home in northern Italy. "That first novel ended with a sea journey aboard a ship called Saturnia; and now in retrospect it almost seems to me that my real passage to Canada came exactly in that fictive voyage, at the point when I had finally been able to fully imagine the place I needed to set out from, since without a point of departure there could be no arrival."[1]

---

[1] Nino Ricci is author of the award-winning novel *The Origin of Species* and of *Lives of the Saints Trilogy*.

A colleague of mine, a passionate journalist of Hindu tradition, had compared the challenge of emigration to the trauma of abandoning one's religion and embracing another. Yet some others call this sense of nationalism the bane of the 21st century.

Tetsuro Shigematsu, a famous TV broadcaster in Vancouver told me a few years ago: "This sense of nationalism is blind sentiment and has nothing to do with right or wrong. I am Japanese genetically, but not Japanese at all. The Japanese wouldn't include me in their definition of the Japanese identity. So what is this thing about identity? I cherish being Canadian, but we keep that to ourselves. This notion of dying for one's country is truly the scourge of this century. This is political nationalism."

That truly is the challenge of change for people landing on their feet in another country, speaking another language, thinking, doing business and worshipping in a custom that is absolutely foreign to the newcomer. It's about appearing Chinese but feeling very Canadian. It's about raising your hand at a citizenship ceremony and swearing allegiance to the Queen, when once you swore allegiance to the soil whose son you were. It's about respecting another set of values, while you keep your own, appearing to integrate and become socially inclusive while feeling alone in a crowd.

Global migration and mobility are today at the heart of global change, impacting on economic and development policy, or human capital, challenging social and political inclusion, religious diversity and the sense of nationhood. This, indeed, is global transformation that calls on governments to review policy in the light of these new emerging conundrums.

So, what really has brought about this human wave of migration and mobility in the last few decades? It's first driven by western countries seeking the best brains in select economic sectors to fuel their economies. A vibrant workforce bumps up the economy and assists countries importing skills to compete in the global market. The other upside to immigration for the recipient country is that growing the population, especially in countries with a high ageing citizenry, raises consumption, lifts the tax base and fires up the economy. So, it's a win, win situation for people choosing to immigrate and for countries looking for talent and skills.

The downside for the recipient country is that sections of its society that are overtly nationalistic do not always welcome newcomers with warm hearts. So one sees confrontations in those specific societies that Samuel Huntington, the American Political Scientist, had called the clash of civilizations. If countrymen are able to embrace our common humanity putting aside the fact of our diversity, then as nations we build a reservoir of the world's great talents.

In ongoing pages, I refer to the unfounded fears of bigots and populists who have sought to introduce legislation that would bar the entry of some religious groups to their shores. In recent times we have seen evidence of this prejudice in European countries including the Netherlands, Hungary, France, Norway and in the United States during the former President Donald Trump's time in the White House.

In April, French President Emmanuel Macron may have scored a victory and grabbed a second term, but he now has to work with a divided country—one part of which had put their weight behind a far right candidate that opposed him.

The divisiveness in national politics and the clash of civilisations is a hindrance to national economic development and I address those issues in the ongoing pages.

CANADA AS A MODEL

Canada is a country of immigrants, and almost everyone recognizes the fact that whether one came to this country three hundred years ago or three months ago, all came to these shores for the same reasons, whether that be poverty from the era of potato famines, political repression during the world wars or the need for a better standard of life.

Canada's early history may have been scarred by stories of land-grabbing, prejudiced treaties with the First Nations, ugly Anglo-French battles and, up until the middle of the 20th century, the perpetuation of race-driven legislation. The segregation of Chinese schools, the isolation of its citizens of Japanese descent after the bombing of Pearl Harbour or the infamous "continuous journey" regulation to bar Indian emigration to Canada are some of those many scars.

With a Charter that guarantees rights and freedoms to all Canadians today, regardless of race or faith, Canada is truly becoming a template for the model state. Its political role on the world stage and its commitment to be a peacekeeper, rather than an aggressor, make it stand out from the comity of nations. It has thrown its weight behind UN conventions that have addressed the problems of war-displaced refugees and is a champion of human rights.

The country's policy makers recognize that immigration is about economics, but there is also a sense that multiculturalism is a work in progress and therefore in the new milieu, our city planners have been brought into the process of creating multicultural cities.

Canada's cities are peaceable – gang wars and riots are uncommon. Some might argue that this is an artificial peace. Other critics say that because people congregate among their own, multiculturalism does not unite, it divides. Be that as it may, multiculturalism is a celebration of Canada's diversity and the many festivals that are hosted in the summer in Toronto, Calgary or Winnipeg represent backdrops against which individuals can participate in the so-called politics of identity.

There is every reason for our city planners to be preoccupied with the fact that newcomers gravitate towards the bigger cities of Montreal, Toronto and Vancouver. The automatic assumption would be that people go to where the jobs are. But research appears not to endorse that view and suggests that familial ties are a greater priority of newcomers to Canada.

Population analysts speak of these residential concentrations as immigrant enclaves and some even say that the key social inclusion issue is poverty.

I think it's correct to say that some groups of immigrants do seek residence in societies that are heterogeneous and that the key social inclusion issue is cultural. Some groups have not formed enclaves at all.

Nonetheless, these new issues are now being examined. Why have these patterns emerged? Is residential concentration caused by exclusion from the mainstream or a conscious choice on the part of ethno-cultural groups to create separate communities?

These issues were, in fact, the engaging focus of immigration conferences that were being hosted in the cities of Canada in the first decade of the 21st century. The need for the host community to become more welcoming societies and the importance of social and political inclusion of all citizens as outlined in Canada's Charter are, even today, preoccupying demographers.

Canada's Charter of Rights and Freedoms guard against any discrimination on the basis of race, or faith or sexual orientation and the Canadian Human Rights Commission acts as the watchdog of those rights. A separate chapter in this book on Race and Religion addresses that question.

STEPPING INTO THE WORKPLACE: THE ACID TEST

The first couple of years for any newcomer to Canada is the acid test. The average observer is likely to define the challenge as one of getting into the workplace because issues about Canadian experience, the competing standards of foreign credentials, and the problems with equivalency assessment act as deterrents. But the test is about resilience.

Pradeep Kharé, a former regional Director General of Environment Canada who told his story of early life in Canada in my book *Canada's Immigrants, Heroes and Countrymen*, says his journey through the early years in Canada had been treacherous, bumpy and full of failures.

"After winning a scholarship from Imperial Oil in 1972, I quit my job in Bombay and travelled to Canada as a student of the University of Saskatchewan to do my master's degree.

"But although I was at the top of my chemical engineering graduating class in India, as a new arrival to Canada, I had to constantly fight the stereotypical notions about immigrants. Going by the adage that you cannot influence the winds but you can certainly adjust your sails, I was able to overcome those disappointments and setbacks by sticking to the long-term goal of fully integrating into Canadian society and reaching my career potential."

Kharé said he quickly realized that in order to succeed in Canada, he would have to learn the so-called "soft skills" such as communication, leadership, strategic thinking, team approach, flexibility and innovation.

"I also discovered quickly that the majority of Canadians are extremely helpful, compassionate, accommodating and genuinely interested in helping underprivileged people like me.

"I aligned myself with such people, ignoring the 'racist' minority, and learned tremendously about the values and cultures of the mainstream society. This was key to my success in Canada."

CANADA BEATS RECORD IN NEWCOMER ARRIVALS

It's obvious that economic globalization is keeping policy makers in developed nations on their guard because it's easy to miss the bus in international competitiveness. The world around us is moving at a dizzy pace. The flow of knowledge, information, goods and people has changed the pathways to economic progress. It is in this milieu that immigration policy is being revamped, prompting city planners to redesign multicultural cities that facilitate social inclusion, religious diversity and the burgeoning of vibrant labour markets. Canada has been ahead of the pack in this big debate.

Public opinion polls conducted in the first decade of this century were reported to have affirmed that the majority of Canadians agree that Canada should continue to be a country that welcomes newcomers and accept the ethnic, racial, religious and linguistic diversity that comes in tow. Consequently, population analysts have been preoccupied with questions about how many newcomers should Canada accept in a calendar year, how should we choose them, and most importantly, how should we ensure that social integration develops.

Of course, there has been a minority opinion as well. At the end of the last century, it was being said that Canadians already are burdened with the problem of the French and English duality and that welcoming the whole world's diversity in this country, exacerbates the challenge of sustaining unity of purpose. But unity of purpose, the majority argue, comes from our common humanity regardless of the diversity of our cultures, and it is within that common humanity that Canada can discover its national identity.

Being a nation of immigrants is, one needs to understand, what makes Canada the country it is. The average Canadian on the street knows very little about immigration and often confuses an immigrant with a migrant. An immigrant chooses to come to another country and make it his home if he qualifies under one of the several immigration programs. The migrant, on the other hand, seeks temporary labour opportunities, and this migrant group as a whole also includes refugees, asylum seekers and displacement populations. So, the common view on the street is that immigration is about Canada's altruism. But it's not. Instead, it's about economic sustainability.

It was being said up until 2015 that at the current economic pace Canada would have to grow its population by, at least, one percent every year to keep economic consumption on the roll, create investment, boost the tax base and meet skills shortages in the knowledge-based economy. That would involve welcoming at least 300,000 immigrants per calendar year, at a time when it was welcoming 225,000 newcomers accounting for 0.7 percent of the country's population.

But in 2021, Canada had well crossed that target and welcomed well over 401,000 new permanent residents. In a news release on 23 December 2021, Sean Fraser, Canada's Minister of Immigration, Refugees and Citizenship declared: "Last year, we set an ambitious goal. Today, we achieved it. This is a historic moment for our country, as we welcome the highest number of newcomers in one year in our history. Canada is built on immigration, and we will continue to welcome the immigrants that Canada needs to succeed. I can't wait to see the incredible contributions that our

401,000 new neighbours make in communities across the country."

The Covid-19 pandemic had virtually upended global migration as a consequence of closed borders and domestic lockdowns. But despite the conundrums, Canada offered shelter to the world's most vulnerable.

A government news statement confirms that today one in three Canadian businesses is owned by an immigrant and one in four health care workers is a newcomer. Business, labour market experts and economists all agree that immigration creates jobs, spurs innovation and helps address labour shortages.

Immigration accounts for almost 100 percent of Canada's labour force growth. Roughly three fourths of Canada's population growth comes from immigration, mostly in the economic category and according to government expectations, in 2036, immigrants will represent up to 30 percent of Canada's population, compared with 20.7 percent in 2011. Indeed, immigration has changed the face of Canada. Today, immigrants make up 37 percent of pharmacists, 36 percent of physicians, 39 percent of dentists, 23 percent of registered nurses, and 35 percent of nurse aides and related occupations.[2]

---

[2] IRCC: Canada welcomes the most immigrants in a

So, while Canada's intake of refugees is altruistic, the country's immigration is driven by economic ambitions. The erstwhile whine about immigrants taking away jobs from Canadians and being a burden on the welfare system has faded away. The image of a lawyer, engineer or doctor driving a taxi is surreal. Indeed, this was the challenge of change, and Canadians have met it head on. The newcomer today is an active participant in our democratic institutions.

MULTICULTURAL CITIES

The first Atlantic Mayors Immigration Conference kicked off in May 2005 at Pier 21 in Halifax, and this was unprecedented in the region at the time, reflecting the new thinking by demographers across the world that cities and communities have a role in developing multi-cultural societies for economic growth.

"The initiative by Atlantic Mayors reflects our recognition of the importance of immigration to long-term economic sustainability and of the need to fill the

---

single year in its history, 23 December 2021.
https://www.canada.ca/en/immigration-refugees-citizenship/news/2021/12/canada-welcomes-the-most-immigrants-in-a-single-year-in-its-history.html.

voids in trades and professional sectors," observed former Halifax Mayor Peter Kelly in his opening address. This new notion of the city and community as catalysts in economic growth sets aside the erstwhile top-down paradigm of governance. Ottawa may set the parameters for national policy, but creating the environments and the infrastructure in which diversity can thrive is a job for city planners and communities.

Professor Sohail Inayatullah, a political scientist, observes: "Historically, the image of the city has gone from the city beautiful, focused on parklands and clean streets to the city ecological. This is the high-tech city, or what one now calls the smart-city - the city that senses and thinks, that can monitor the needs of its citizens - when trees are about to interfere with power lines, when criminals are about to loot a store."[3] Geneva, he says, has taken a different tack. "What was once a classical, traditionally white Euro city, has in the last thirty or forty years, transformed beyond belief."

I have had the opportunity to see that new smart city. It now has a credible multicultural face with cafes lined with African, middle-eastern, Italian, Indian and

---

[3] Sohail Inayatullah is an Australian academic and a Professor at the Graduate Institute of Futures Studies at Tamkang University in Taipei, Taiwan.

fast food restaurants and in public life one sees a slew of cultures mixing.

But what is a multicultural city? Inayatullah observes: "First it means city spaces are not segregated by race or gender, one should not be able to identify an ethnic area, or at least not see it in a negative way. Second, citizens should feel they are part of the city, that they are not discriminated against, especially by those in authority. But a multicultural city is also about incorporating other ways of knowing, of creating a complex and chaotic model of space, such that the city does not necessarily match the values of only one culture - mosques with temples and banks. City design not only done by trained city planners but as well by feng shui experts, searching for the energy lines."

The need for vibrant social inclusion that will create the climate in which social capital can develop while pre-empting the mushrooming of ghettos of people of like cultures has fuelled debate across Canada. The importance of religion as an aspect of diversity has been increasing too, since ultimately, ideological differences related to religious principles may prove more intractable than the racial divide which presently concerns policymakers.

IMMIGRATION: IS IT THE LIFE AND
DEATH OF CANADIAN SOCIETY?

"How we respond to the challenges of immigration, diversity and population change will literally determine whether we as a society live or die." That was a somewhat shocking statement made some time ago by Brian Lee Crowley, the founding President of the Atlantic Institute for Market Studies (AIMS).

Others have said it differently. John Ibbitson, of the *Globe and Mail,* had ruffled feathers, some years ago, with his column: "Why Atlantic Canada remains white and poor."

The people of Atlantic Canada at the turn of this century were grappling with the complexities of change in the region's demographics. It had witnessed an exodus of its youth leave for greener pastures as a consequence of its failure to recruit even a fraction of its share of immigrants. A high ageing population and out-migration were contributing to a sharp decline in the region's share of Canada's population.

So, Crowley at the time, posed the question: "What is it about us that we cannot keep our youth, draw newcomers, or keep more than a third of those who do come? Growing immigration is a sure sign of economic and cultural dynamism," he said. "But immigrants don't have to come here, and indeed have largely stopped coming."

He was making the point that while governments can make a difference, immigration is not merely an affair of governments. It depends, at least, as much on host societies to keep newcomers in their provinces.

The greater part of the industrialized world faces very significant labour shortages today and in the future. That, and not unemployment, is this region's chief public policy challenge, Crowley said.

"Most industries, including the fisheries, are forecasting significant challenges finding workers in the near future. Doing what is right for Atlantic Canadians will also be the right thing for attracting immigrants, including a reduced tax burden, a culture of education, a lightening of the regulatory burden, especially on newcomers' access to many regulated professions."

Jeffrey Reitz of the University of Toronto, speaking at a forum at Saint Mary's University in Halifax some years ago, spoke of the need for a strong commitment to large-scale immigration and to negotiate higher targets as a first step. But he also made the point that while Canada's "points" system as a criteria for entry was designed to woo the brightest and the best, second centres like the cities of Atlantic Canada will have to expect lower levels of skills. That's because today's immigrants tend to pile up in the bigger cities because of labour demand, city size and family ties.

Reitz had advised some caution. "The immigration of unskilled people can cause immigrant poverty. We must pursue skills selectively in large scale immigration and that should benefit the economy."

As any immigrant knows, uprooting and moving on to lands of different cultures is not music to the ears. It can be traumatic. A great majority of newcomers talk of loneliness in the initial years of settlement and later of the lack of a sense of belonging. Crowley addressed that observation in an OpEd he wrote for my newspaper *Touch BASE*.

"Immigration is not chiefly a matter of jurisdiction, but of people and therefore of the heart," he wrote. "Immigrants are people who uproot themselves from their homes in search of a better life. Thus immigrants tend to congregate in specific cities. People don't move to places they've never heard of, so one of the most powerful attractions for immigrants is whether there are people like them in a new community — people who have prospered there.

"Being made to feel wanted and welcome is thus the strongest pro-immigration policy there is. So, in order for immigration to move outside the big cities, we need to foster immigrant communities, and not just individual immigrants."

POLICING IN A
MULTICULTURAL SOCIETY

Over the last decade, the police have come under fire from allegations of racial bias, and although there is great debate on whether or not racism has touched the cornerstone of the Canadian criminal justice system, there is consensus among academics and justice officials that the perception of bias is widespread. Indeed, survey research consistently reveals that the majority of Canada's minority residents perceive discrimination in policing.

In an interview with Halifax Police Chief Jean-Michel Blais in 2018, I asked if there was any truth in the widespread notion that African Nova Scotians and aboriginals are over-represented in our prisons. Chief Blais admitted to that notion being true. "Yes. African Nova Scotians and aboriginals are unfortunately still over-represented in our prisons as compared to their respective populations, not only here in Nova Scotia, but throughout Canada," he said. "Historical issues around poverty, education, health and marginalization have all contributed to this."

Statistics from the Office of the Correctional Investigator, reveal that indigenous people are vastly over-represented and account for a rising share in the Canadian prison system, making up 30.04 percent of the offender population in 2020, while representing only 4.9 percent of the total population.[4] The most recent data from Canada's federal correctional agency indicate that Black people accounted for 7.2 percent of federal offenders in 2018/2019 while comprising 3.5 percent of Canada's population.[5]

In Halifax, some years ago, Black Nova Scotian boxer Kirk Johnson filed a complaint with the Nova Scotia Human Rights Commission of harassment by the police. The Commission weighed the evidence, found a prima facie case was made out and referred the complaint to a board of inquiry. The courts finally ruled in Johnson's favour. The police, nonetheless, insist that the criminal justice system is colour blind.

In response to these allegations of discrimination, civilian oversight of the police was proposed as one method for correcting this perception of discrimination, improving the relationship between the police

---

[4] "Indigenous People in Federal Custody Surpasses 30 percent". Office of the Correctional Investigator. Retrieved 4 July 2020.

[5] Maheux & Do, 2019; Public Safety Canada, 2020.

and the community and increasing accountability within the criminal justice system.

At the end of the last century, most police jurisdictions in Canada shifted from an enforcement model to a community responsive service model, in response to several issues including an emerging focus on race relations, allegations of police discrimination, and public disillusionment.

Valerie J. Pruegger, a cross-cultural organizational psychologist, told me some years ago: "Community policing is an attempt to move away from an isolated and detached model where police rarely interact with the community except in response to a complaint, to one where the police are seen to be part of the community in which they serve."

But the move to creating partnerships between police and the community does not come without resistance. A number of internal and external barriers exist to developing community policing or police/community partnership models.

Pruegger says: "One of the main barriers can be resistance and resentment from police officers who see it as an erosion of their powers and their ability to act with relative autonomy and anonymity. Many police officers are vested in their roles as crime fighters, warriors against crime, and cherish an image of the tough law enforcer."[6]

At a seminar hosted in Halifax some years ago, police officers shared notes with their audiences and affirmed that moving to community policing has called for a new set of skills for police officers. This has led to increased education standards and a wider pool of candidates from which to draw. That recruitment pool includes the best and brightest from Canadian universities and from non-traditional groups in the community: Aboriginal, Asian, South Asian, and others. This allows police services to better reflect the community in which they serve and enhances their ability to form effective partnerships.

HALIFAX POLICE WORKS
WITH DIVERSE COMMUNITIES

Police Chief Jean-Michel Blais, told me that a recent CBC study found that the Halifax Regional Police is the only Canadian police service that fully represents the community it serves. "We achieved this through active recruiting initiatives which continue to this day,"

---

[6] Valerie Pruegger, PhD, is a cross-cultural organizational Psychologist.

Chief Blais said. "Our goal will be to supplement our ranks with cadets from diverse demographics as well as women, who unfortunately are the most under-represented group in policing today."

The RCMP and the Halifax Regional Police took the lead some years ago to set up a Cultural Diversity Committee (CDC) composed of people from several faith groups and ethnic communities. The objective was obvious. The police today work amidst a more culturally diverse community and recognize the need to know these communities, the race, religion and language, in order to be more sensitized to their custom and tradition and the issues they may be confronted with.

The demographic today is, of course, changing rapidly. Arabic is the third most spoken language after English and French in the Halifax area. The city has seen a marked increase in diversity and with it the emergence of many diasporic communities and faith groups. "In order to respond effectively, the Equity Diversity Officer's role has had to evolve to ensure that our various diasporic, minority and marginalized commu-nities have a connection point to their police service," he said.

Crime rates have been slowly dropping as a result of better policing. However, Chief Blais says that "crime may have simply morphed from an in-person activity to an online one. As a result, crime may just have migrated in a higher proportion to the online sphere."

Interface between police officers and our communities is now common.

Sgt Scott, an officer of the police force told me some time ago, that there is already open communication lines with the Jewish and Islamic communities and through seminars with them the police are getting familiar with their customs and worship practice. He said the Maritime Sikh Society has invited several of them to the Gurdwara to join in their grieving process as well.

On the Cultural Diversity Committee of the Halifax Regional Police today are Bahá'is, Muslims, Jews, Sikhs, Egyptian Coptics and people from various communities including the Vietnamese, Chinese, Lebanese, African Nova Scotians and Aboriginal communities. This committee, I was told, was able to oversee the screening practices at airports—which some newcomers suspect are sometimes discriminatory—and have those misconceptions dispelled.

SOCIAL AND POLITICAL INCLUSION

Dr. Godwin Eni, a Nigerian physiotherapist, fled Nigeria in the throes of an ugly civil war and got to Lagos airport by the seat of his pants. He arrived in Montreal on October 6, 1970, with a bullet lodged in his armpit and 50 Pounds Sterling in his pocket. It was the time when the FLQ, the terrorist group, had kidnapped the British Trade Commissioner in Montreal. The mood outside the airport was tense with military tanks on alert. Three days later, anyway, he arrived in Saskatoon and took up assignment at the University Hospital.

The experience with Mrs X, his very first patient in Canada, was traumatic and unforgettable, he told me. "I was assigned to provide her with breathing exercises and vasodilatation. But at my very sight, the lady screamed and yelled and all that hysteria got the nurses scurrying to her bedside. In the first couple of minutes since walking up to her bedside, I did not know what was going on. I was told later, Mrs X had never before seen a Black man. She had been raised in a rural town on the Manitoba-Saskatchewan border."

Dr. Eni told me he felt humiliated and inferior. He told the Head of Rehabilitation Medicine that same day that he was returning to Nigeria.

Keep in mind, this occurred in 1970. Notwithstanding that fact, you realize that ignorance of the diversity of the human race, customs and traditions of people originating from a spectrum of different cultures, can bring about social exclusion which makes societal integration and a sense of nationhood almost impossible.

So, the results of the Canadian Heritage Ethnic Diversity Survey conducted a few years ago should not surprise you. The results indicate that we have yet to find a way for newcomers who identify with minority ethnic and racial groups to feel included in everyday community life. It turned out that 36 percent of respondents reported they had experienced discrimination. The survey found that 50 percent of Blacks, 43 percent of Japanese and 35 percent of South Asians reported the beguiling experience of a concealed prejudice, occurring mostly in the workplace, in stores, on the street and when dealing with the courts or the police.

In *New Poverty in Canada*, Abdolmohammed Kazemipur and Shiva Halli argue that there is a "new poverty" in Canada that is concentrated in selected neighborhoods that are often associated with Aboriginal or recently settled immigrant populations. They believe that emerging ghettos may precipitate a culture of poverty wherein residents see no means of improving their livelihood and instead become passive recipients of the welfare state.[7]

In the first decade of the 21st century, some immigration analysts had expressed the view that there are increasing concentrations of people from the same cultural and linguistic background in Canadian metropolitan areas with significant levels of poverty because of their relative lack of marketable skills and of English and French language proficiency. They speculate that these ghettos trap residents and their children into long term poverty and might even lead to social conflict.

In my view, social exclusion may perhaps be connected with poverty, but racial prejudice plays its part in perpetuating exclusion. In the 21st century, we see affluent immigrant groups settling in Canada and yet these people may confirm that they have been made to feel socially excluded.

But as Dr. Howard Duncan, Chair Emeritus, International Metropolis Project and Former Editor of International Migration observes in a note to me: "As many societies in the West experience population age-

---

[7] Abdolmohammed Kazemipur and Shiva Halli—*New Poverty in Canada: Ethnic Groups and Ghetto Neighbourhoods.*

ing, their governments, recognizing that increasing birth rates is not feasible, are turning to immigration to bolster their labour forces, enhance innovation and productivity, and increase or simply maintain their population size.

"Any society that is to have a successful immigration program will need simultaneously to have a successful means of settling and integrating newcomers in their societies. Without successful integration, large scale immigration will not provide the benefits that the government envisioned. In part, this is a matter of social justice, of offering newcomers meaningful inclusion in their new societies.

But it is also straightforward economics. Excluding newcomers from a place in their new society reduces their ability to contribute to the labour market, to provide the innovation that diversity is said to promise, and to put their entrepreneurial spirit to practice.

"Investing in immigration is only a first step. The real work comes with integration, and this must be practiced daily if a country is to succeed both economically and socially."[8]

---

[8] Dr. Howard Duncan, Chair Emeritus, International Metropolis Project, and Former Editor of *International Migration*.

A point to note, however, is that social exclusion is a deterrent to the creation of social capital which is the basis of a society's prosperity. In other words, social inclusion generates increased social capital and social exclusion works the other way around, reducing the level of trust required for a vibrant economy and a well-functioning society.

So, if we know what's good for us, we must choose to come together as a society and design multicultural city spaces that do not segregate by race or gender, nor identify an ethnic area, as Professor Inyatullah observes in the foregoing pages.

In 2021, Canada hailed its acceptance of 401,000 newcomers as a historical moment for the country. These newcomers make up the educated, business and professional class only, and policy makers are not daunted by the sheer scale of numbers, nor do they invoke fears like those voiced by anti-immigration groups in Europe. Social inclusion is key to the creation of peaceable societies that thrive with an understanding that despite our diverse cultures, it's our common humanity that allows nationhood to flourish.

REFUGEES: WHY DO PEOPLE MIGRATE

Speaking plainly, I think the one reason why people migrate is because people are drawn to where the jobs are. The widening of gaps in opportunity that lie in the cities and are virtually absent in the rural areas of the less developed countries, separate the privileged from the poor. So, people move to where the jobs are within one's country's borders or outside it and are grouped in the category of migrant labour.

But the other scary side to migration is that people move not out of choice but actually flee for the safety of their lives. These are people who are internally displaced in their own countries or seeking asylum and refugee status in foreign lands.

The 1951 Geneva Convention on Refugees is a United Nations multilateral treaty that defines who a refugee is and sets out the rights of individuals who are granted asylum and the responsibilities of nations that grant asylum.

The UN defines a refugee as someone who has a well-founded fear of being persecuted for reasons of race, religion, nationality, membership of a particular social group or political opinion; is outside the country of his nationality and is unable or, owing to such fear, is unwilling to avail himself of the protection of that country; or who, not having a nationality and being outside the country of his former habitual residence as a result of such events, is unable or, owing to such fear, is unwilling to return to it.

Migrant statistics therefore must be distinguished from stats relating to the international movement of immigrants who choose to leave a country and settle in another if they meet the criteria set out by welcoming countries in respect of education, financial status, health and good conduct.

Major migration and displacement of people are a consequence of political instability and war. The late 20th and the early 21st centuries have seen a stream of refugees fleeing war in their countries - some examples being the Iran-Iraq conflict, the Gulf War, the civil wars in Syria, Egypt, Libya and Yemen, the Bosnian War, strife in the Congo, the Central African Republic, South Sudan, extreme violence that drove Myanmar's Rohingya populations to seek refuge in Bangladesh, the political instability in Venezuela and other Latin American countries, and most recently the Russia-Ukraine war.

But the waves of human mobility that streamed across borders after World War II and later the exodus of refugees fleeing conflict and strife in the Middle East, Africa and Latin America were probably unprecedented. It challenged Europe's border surveillance and its capacity for human compassion, uncovering racial prejudice from small sections of society driven by a handful of populists and demagogues with right-wing nationalist dreams.

At the end of 2015, the world sat up and took notice again. Alan Kurdi, the Syrian child fleeing the country's war was found dead on a shore in Europe after a migrant boat capsized.

World leaders were stunned, and compassion burst open the flood gates to a migrant flow into Europe unprecedented since World War II. That appeared like a moment of truth when the world was putting aside prejudice in the race to save masses of humanity. The tragedy pulled at the heart strings of European leaders, led by Germany's Angela Merkel, who opened the country's border wide enough to take in at least 31,000 migrants and refugees over the September 5 weekend.

But in the midst of this crisis, Australia's former Prime Minister Tony Abbot, who was unceremoniously ousted from office mid-September 2015, told European leaders that the way to stop the crisis was to "stop the boats." Apart from that being immoral migration policy, it reflected an immature understanding of the gravity of this crisis.

Later, on the weekend of 20 September, Austria was challenged with the arrival of another 17,000 migrants. In their desperation, Hungarian forces resorted to tear gas to disperse the crowds. There were rumblings of dissent at the time. Hungary's populist Prime Minister Viktor Orban had claimed for months that Europe was being overrun by refugees who threaten to overwhelm its economy and security and alter its very culture and identity. "Those arriving have been raised in another religion and represent a radically different culture. Most of them are not Christians but Muslims," Mr. Orban wrote in a commentary for *Frankfurt Allgemeine Zeitung*, a German newspaper.

But the Lutheran Immigration and Refugee Service group was quick to sensitise the European world, saying: "As people of faith we do not stand for welcome on the condition that refugees are Christian. We stand for welcome because we are Christian."

Hungary was, indeed, being urged to halt its campaign portraying refugees as 'invaders'. The Danish parliament had, at the time, passed a package of measures to deter refugees from seeking asylum, including confiscating valuables to pay for their stay, despite protests from international human rights organizations.

The bill which allowed the confiscation of refugees' cash exceeding 10,000 Kroner had prompted comparisons to Nazi Germany's confiscation of the personal possessions of Jews in World War II.

A record 1.3 million migrants applied for asylum in the 28 member states of the European Union, Norway and Switzerland in 2015 – nearly double the previous high water mark of roughly 700,000 that was set in 1992 after the fall of the Iron Curtain and the collapse of the Soviet Union, according to a Pew Research Center analysis of data from Eurostat, the European Union's statistical agency.[9]

Europe was convulsed with this flow of migrants which pushed European states to take divisive positions on the refugee policy, resulting in some closing borders with far-right European political movements, promoting distrust of Muslims, and white-nationalist conspiracy theorists predicting a Muslim take-over of Europe.

A conversation on refugees and asylum seekers often begins with statistics. That's the unkindest cut of all. But, of course, I understand that stats tell a story and

---

[9] pewresearch.org/global/2016/08/02/ Pew Research Center, Washington, D.C. (August 2, 2016).

paint a picture of the gravity of the crisis. That being said, I end this chapter with some numbers:

At the end of 2020, at least 82.4 million people were forcibly displaced worldwide as a result of conflict, persecution, human rights violations and violence. That staggering figure has included 26.4 million refugees, 48.0 million internally displaced people, 4.1 million asylum-seekers, and 3.9 million Venezuelans displaced abroad.[10]

What's the way out?

Education is key to ending the unbridled flow of migrant labour from villages to towns. It moderates migration and the movement of people outside their national borders because the jobs in a literate society can be found in the home country. It holds out the hope that literate societies will abhor war in the future and that the morality of nations will engender a society that embraces peace so that people may never have to flee their countries and seek refuge in foreign lands as they do now in warring countries.

---

[10] UNHCR: Global Trends: Forced Displacement in 2020. https://www.unhcr.org/flagship-reports/global-trends/

CHAPTER III

RACE AND RELIGION

Racism is as old as the hills. I am no historian, so I am not going to take you down the road in history when it first raised its ugly head. But we can look at an ugly past briefly to get a sense of what the scourge was like through the last couple of centuries, the damage it had done, the peoples and nations it had separated, the riots, massacres and the Holocaust it ignited.

So, what is racism? It is the belief that different races possess distinct characteristics, capabilities, or qualities, especially so as to distinguish them as inferior or superior to one another. Into this definition gamut, fall reactions of prejudice, the practice of discrimination, notions of xenophobia, segregation and supremacism and in the political arena, the creation of systems like apartheid.

It is a relatively modern concept arising in the European age of imperialism, the subsequent growth of capitalism and through the era of the Atlantic Slave Trade. It was a major force behind racial segregation in the US in the 19th and early 20th centuries as well as in South Africa under apartheid.[1]

The scourge of racism has played a defining role in the Armenian and Serb genocides, the Holocaust, the European colonization of Africa and Asia and the Soviet deportation of indigenous minorities. White supremacy prevailed in the US from its founding up until the civil rights movement.

In 1939, when history's most brutal cataclysm broke out, some 60-85 million people perished. Nazi Germany, as part of a deliberate program of extermination, systematically killed over 11 million people including six million Jews. Adolf Hitler, the chief antagonist in World War II, did this to quench his desire for a pure Aryan race in Europe.

South Africa has had its share of race-based violence from the post-World War II era up until the 1960s. The Durban riots which broke out between 13 and 15 January 1949 were an organized pogrom fought primarily by Black South Africans targeting Indians and South Africans of Indian Origin.[2] Then, shortly after

---

[1] Fredrickson, George M. 1988. The arrogance of race: historical perspectives on slavery, racism, and social inequality. Middletown, Conn: *Wesleyan University Press* <https://en.wikipedia.org/wiki/ Racism>

[2] Tolsi, Niren (19 July 2021). "KwaZulu-Natal races

World War II, the South African National Party took control of the government of South Africa and imposed an apartheid regime, separating whites and non-whites. On March 21, 1960, South Africa's police in cold blood shot 70 Black peaceful protesters on the streets of Sharpville.

The world again sat up and took notice. The random shooting was a wake up call, and in 1966 the UN declared March 21 as the International Day for the Elimination of Racial Discrimination.

What good did that do? The world tucked it under the carpet and moved on. Six years later, in 1972, Ugandan President Idi Amin ethnically cleansed Uganda's Asians giving them 90 days to leave the country.[3]

In the 21st century, a nationalistic culture again took root on European soil as the waves of migrants billowed and racial prejudice got deep seated. On 22 July 2011, Norwegian terrorist Anders Behring Breivik, in a shooting and bombing rampage murdered 92 people. He said that he did this because the number of Muslims in Western Europe was "reaching critical mass" and that

---

back to 1949". Mail & Guardian. Retrieved 16 Nov 2021. https://en.wikipedia.org/wiki/Durban_riots

[3] 1972: Asians given 90 days to leave Uganda. BBC.

"there is a core of Cultural Communist elites in Western Europe who really want to destroy Western civilization, European traditions, national solidarity and Christianity." Breivik portrayed himself as a modern-day Crusader, fighting against what he sees as the Islamic invasion of Europe.

The knife-edge of racial prejudice has since been blunted. But the Oslo massacre is a reminder that the scourge of racism is not dead. Racial prejudice raises its ugly head at the slightest provocation in European cities.

A row over France's crackdown on Roma migrants from Romania and Bulgaria dominated a summit of EU leaders in Brussels some years ago. President Nicolas Sarkozy was furious after European Justice Commissioner Viviane Reding appeared to compare France's removal of Roma people with Gypsy deportations during World War II. She compared France's actions to the persecution of Jews and Gypsies in Nazi-occupied France, when she said: "This is a situation I had thought Europe would not have to witness again after the Second World War."[4]

---

[4] "French ministers fume after Reding rebuke over Roma". BBC. September 15, 2010. Archived from the original on September 16, 2010. Retrieved 2010-09-16.

Indeed, the world has come a long way from the days of the import of slave labour. It has taken the courage of men like Abraham Lincoln who freed slaves and Martin Luther King and Malcolm X who led the civil rights movement in the United States and women including Rosa Parks who worked to break loose from the perverted ideology that drives divisiveness in our societies.

A sinister side to this racist culture has been unfolding, since the early decade of the 21st century, rolling back globalization. That was evident in the Brexit call to "take back control" and Donald Trump's mantra of "Making America Great Again." The emergence of populists and demagogues especially in Britain, the Netherlands and the United States impacted on global society and that was scary.

In his campaign, Trump promised to bar the entry of Muslims, build a wall to stop the Mexicans whom he allegedly accused of being rapists and druggies, and immediately terminate President Obama's "executive amnesties" so as to put America first.

Trump's campaign had already found favour with Dutch politician Geert Wilders who had set out proposals ahead of the 2017 elections in the Netherlands, which included banning migrants from Islamic countries and closing mosques, Islamic schools and asylum centres.

Canada has had its dark days as well. The Shelburne riots in July 1784, fought between white landless Loyalist veterans of the American War of Independence and Black Loyalists in the town of Shelburne in the province of Nova Scotia, have been characterized as the first race riots in Canada, and one of the earliest recorded race riots in North America.[5]

Later in1886, when riots broke out between white settlers and Chinese "coolies" brought to Canada to work on the Canadian Pacific Railway, a "Chinese Head Tax" was introduced to halt immigration from China. In 1907, riots broke out in Vancouver targeting Chinese and Japanese businesses and the Asiatic Exclusion League was formed to drive the Chinese and Japanese out of the province.

The racial riots, the deportation of Indians on the Komagata Maru, who challenged an amendment to the Immigration Act in 1908, and the refusal to accept Jews on the St. Louis in 1939, who later perished in Auschwitz, are some of those early memories that have stained Canada's history.

---

[5] "The Shelburne Race Riots". The Canadian Encyclopedia. Retrieved September 2, 2019.

In recent times, racism has raised its ugly head in several cities of Canada. Viola Desmond, a Canadian Black woman was ordered out of the Whites-only area of the Roseland Theatre in New Glasgow, Nova Scotia, in 1946. The incident challenged racial segregation in Canada and prompted a human rights debate in the country nine years before the Rosa Parks incident in the US. Her case is one of the most publicized incidents of racial discrimination in Canadian history and helped start the modern civil rights movement in Canada.

A few months ago on January 31, 2022, the Canadian Race Relations Foundation (CRRF) put out a statement that said: "There must be no ambiguity about where we stand. The trucker convoy in Ottawa, had put many in a state of fear because of what they witnessed this past weekend. The display of Confederate flags, Nazi symbols, and the racially-charged harassment of people of colour and religious minorities being carried out are all wrong and deserving of the strongest of condemnations."

But this narrative is incomplete without a reference to injustices meted out to Canada's First Nations. Senator Murray Sinclair, former Chair of the Truth and Reconciliation Commission of Canada, told a packed auditorium at Saint Mary's University in March 2017, of Canada's residential schools which were set up to take indigenous children away from their families and induct them in schools to indoctrinate them in another culture, for the purpose of eliminating the first racial group. He said that was an act of genocide and referenced Article 2E of the UN Commission on Genocide that was passed in 1949.

The bane of racism is no more black and white. It's tentacles reach far and wide. It is also far from dead. The struggle against it is, in fact, a matter of priority for the world community. It occurs on a daily basis, hindering progress of millions of people around the world, denying individuals the basic principles of equality, fueling ethnic hatred which eventually leads to genocide – all of which can destroy lives and fracture communities.

But Canada has demonstrated remorse and its governments in the 21st century have made amends with apologies for several wrongs. The last segregated Black school in Merlin, Ontario, was finally closed in 1965, and elsewhere segregated schools were phased out around the same time, with the last segregated school in Canada closing in 1983.

It has made federal apologies for the internment of the Japanese in World War II; the imposition of the Head Tax on Chinese immigrants between 1885 and 1923; Canada's residential schools in which more than

150,000 First Nations, Metis and Innuit children were inducted between 1840 and 1996; the deportation in April 1914 of Indians on the Komagata Maru and a few others.

On April 15, 2010, Viola Desmond received an apology from Nova Scotia Premier Darrell Dexter and was granted a free pardon at a historic event at Province House sixty four years after she was arrested for sitting in the whites-only section of a movie theatre in New Glasgow, Nova Scotia.

In February 2010, Halifax Council ratified the Africville Apology, and the Government of Canada announced $250,000 for the Africville Heritage Trust to design a museum and build a replica of the community church. Africville was a small community of predominantly Black Canadians located in Halifax. It developed on the southern shore of Bedford Basin and existed from the early 1800s to the 1960s. In January 1964, Halifax City Council voted to authorize the relocation of Africville residents.

Halifax Mayor Peter Kelly said it appropriately while making an apology to the African Nova Scotian community. "Our history cannot be rewritten, but thankfully, the future is a blank page, and starting today, we hold the pen with which we can write a shared tomorrow," he said.

Indeed, in this shared tomorrow, the world will strive to increase its share of the world's intellect and skills to boost its economy and stay competitive. If it does not, its economies are at risk of decline. In other words, a shared future is what all of us on the planet must seek going forward. So, while an apology does not erase the wrongs, it softens the blows on whom those wrongs were inflicted. Indeed, the future is a blank page and it is on that page we all seek to write a shared tomorrow.

In a hard-hitting speech some time ago, Zeid Ra'ad Al Hussein, the former UN High Commissioner for Human Rights, warned against the impact that populists and demagogues would have and called for the safeguard of human rights law. He was speaking at a gala of the Peace, Justice and Security Foundation in The Hague.

In his concluding remarks he asked: "Are we going to continue to stand by and watch this banalization of bigotry, until it reaches its logical conclusion? Ultimately, it is the law that will safeguard our societies – human rights law, binding law which is the distillation of human experience, of generations of human suffering, the screams of the victims of past crimes and hate. We must guard this law passionately and be guided."

THE CHALLENGE OF RELIGIOUS
DIVERSITY

This narrative, as well, is told from a Canadian perspective.

There is a sense among people of faith that religion and interfaith conversations can become the critical solution to today's grave problems. Hate, intolerance, tyranny and violence have no place in a world that's looking to create for itself peaceful societies. But as people of different faiths take up residence in the West – and that will happen because immigration spurs economic growth – the challenge of accommodating religious diversity, especially within the framework of secular governance gets more pointed.

That nations are struggling with ways to accommodate religious diversity is witnessed at large. In Canada, for example, it is witnessed in the very public debates, some years ago, over the funding of religious schools, the call for faith-based arbitration or the introduction of Muslim Sharia law into the country's penal code, the lobbying by a section of Ontario's Hindus for a waterway designated for traditional burial rituals and a call for the establishment of a commission in Quebec looking into reasonable accommodation of diverse cultural practices focused on religious diversity.

So, between 2011 and 2016, I convened three Spiritual Diversity Conferences in Halifax that saw delegates and religious scholars converge on the city from across North America to address the challenges of our time – the injustices within our global society, the social inequality, the racial prejudice, moral and ethical issues that divide us as a people.

These conferences were designed to seek commonalities as well as acknowledge differences and make a commitment to engage in civil discourse. The hope was to promote greater interfaith understanding with people affirming a respect for the religious beliefs of others, promoting egalitarianism and affirming respect at the same time for Canada's core democratic values.

Canada has confronted these challenges fairly well up to this point. But as the reality of pluralism gets deep seated, the challenge will be greater. I say greater because I believe public opinion surveys reveal that relations between faith communities and secular Canadians are now a very important preoccupation. There is a significant demographic change in the country – characterized by considerable growth in the percentage of Canadians who are not Christian as well as an increase in Canadians reporting no religion. There is already evidence of an exponential growth in religions from South and East Asia, Africa and the Middle East.

According to the country's 2001 census, the count of Muslims in Canada was 579,740 at the time, which was roughly two percent of the population. But by 2019 the Muslim head count had crossed the million mark to account for 3.7 percent of the population.[6]

In the late 20th and early 21st centuries, large numbers of Muslims immigrated to Western Europe. By 2010, an estimated 44 million Muslims were resident in Europe, including an estimated 19 million in the EU. By 2030, they are projected to compose eight percent of the population or 58 million people.[7]

September 11 and its subsequent war on terror raised questions including what triggered the attack on New York's twin towers and how can our societies going forward work on a paradigm shift from the inevitable clash of civilizations to a dialogue of civilizations.

---

[6] Statistics Canada, 2011 National Household Survey profile <www12.statscan.gc.ca> Retrieved April 4, 2019. This does not constitute an endorsement by Statistics Canada.

[7] Grim, Brian J.; Karim, Mehtab S. (January 2011). "The Future of the Global Muslim Population: Projections for 2010-2030" (PDF). The Pew Forum on Religion & Public Life. Washington, D.C.: Pew Research Center. LCCN 2011505325.Archived (PDF) from the original on 14 October 2018. Retrieved 21 January 2021.

It's very obvious that these new challenges to western societies have emerged as the need to grow economies have pushed governments to look for steady growth in their populations as well as production skills through immigration. But the hundreds of thousands of newcomers that are headed to countries in the West every year are not going to leave their religion at the door and come in. How then, do we accommodate religious diversity in a secular framework of governance?

The importance of religion as one aspect of diversity has been gaining ground and the need for concomitant research or policy capacity to address many of the issues that arise from religious diversity is recognised.

In the aftermath of the 9/11 crisis, the "clash of civilizations" hypothesis of American political scientist Samuel Huntington had re-emerged. In the United States and Canada, popular discourse had come to accept a direct linkage between religion and terrorism. Critics argued that Islam had been unfairly singled out ignoring other manifestations of terrorism including the bombing of an Air India carrier by Canadian-Sikh separatists in June 1985; the Oklahoma City bombing a decade later by a white supremacist and the troubles in Northern Ireland. Nevertheless, the common view that religion and terrorism are connected became harder to dislocate.

The arrest of Maher Arar, a Canadian of Syrian descent, by the US government and his subsequent despatch to Syria where he was tortured, opened a storm of debate in Canada about the need for a balance between liberty and state security. The clamour by human rights groups in Canada worked its way up to have Arar ultimately released and brought back to Canada.

Canada recognizes the new challenge that it's up against and that religious diversity is intrinsically part of the package that multiculturalism brings.

So, is religion the cause of it all or does religion have a role to play in transforming a violent world into a peaceful one? Where does hatred lie? Can religion help? On the other hand, do world religions have a perspective on human rights? Do the founding populations in Western countries see Muslims as different from themselves? Can we bring spirituality into the workplace and in everyday life? How do ethnic communities identify with their faith traditions across Europe and North America or anywhere else where migrants take up residence?

Our population analysts may want to address these questions because our economies have come to rely on new skills and intellect and a steady growth in population. The battle is not quite really between religions but between the aggressively secular and the religious.

Fr. Raymond J. de Souza, Pastor of the Sacred Heart of Mary Parish in Ontario, delivering the keynote address at the 2011 Spiritual Diversity Conference in Halifax said this: "The growth of secular fundamentalism in public life can be successful in marginalizing religious voices, but at the risk of radicalization."

IDENTITY POLITICS

The Dilemma of Protecting Religious Freedom was the topic of the Marshall Lecture in Public Philosophy delivered at Saint Mary's University in Halifax in 2014 by Dr. Avigail Eisenberg, professor of Political Science at the University of Victoria.[8]

She spoke of conflicts on the subject that have surfaced lately and which have become the backdrop to the dialogue. She pointed to polygamy within the Mormon cultures, the Sikh custom of wearing the kirpan, the conflict about the headscarf in France, ritual animal slaughter in Spain and offensive cartoons. The

---

[8] CCEPA: (Canadian Centre for Ethics in Public Affairs) Marshall Lecture - *Dilemmas of Protecting Religious Freedom* - Dr. Avigail Eisenberg. July 18, 2014.

questions on the table included: Is polygamy an excuse or legitimate religious practice? Is the display of the kirpan, real or symbolic?

"We see a new era of identity politics where groups advance claims before institutions in order to contain one's identity," Dr. Eisenberg said. "So, as a result, linguistic and religious minorities have become politicized and mobilized on the basis of gender, race, language, indigeneity, religion, ethnicity and sexuality. They have confronted restrictions because they are discriminatory."

She thinks there are two reactions to this kind of politics. Normative political theorists are generally sympathetic to identity politics because it leads to the advancement of human rights. On the other hand, recognition of identity is a way to respect others and track social exclusion of immigrant minorities.

"But empirical scholarship holds the view that political movements are rarely seen to be spontaneous expressions of social injustice. Identity claims are often distorted by power dynamics between groups," she contends. "The problems connected with identity politics are social fragmentation, stereotyping, entrenching elite power within groups, encouraging patriarchy and the fact that minorities are offered modest reforms."

Dr. Eisenberg said: "Identity politics encourages people to mobilize on the basis of what distinguishes them rather than unites them and it undermines social trust." She believes there are risks in identity politics, which is why some propose public institutions should discourage claims of identity.

But how has this era of identity politics changed in Canada? Since 1982, constitutional protection speaks to the issues of identity politics and to the protection of conscience and religion. Many sections of the Charter do, in fact, speak to the protection of indigenous rights. So there are challenges.

There is one way to view how identity politics has impacted on the way freedom of religion is interpreted, she says. "Consider the Lord's Day Act which was struck down in 1985. The argument was that the law does not impede anyone from choosing nor does the law deny freedom of religion. Laws that privilege the practice of one religion over another, violate freedom of religion."

Dr. Eisenberg contends that the good thing about identity politics is that it puts aside social exclusion and uses it to trace discrimination. The risks are that when you treat identity politics as non-negotiable, there is the possibility of deepening hierarchies within the groups. "By validating the veil, Muslim girls will want to practice veiling and escalate orthodoxy. You see this in divorce and polygamy cases," she affirms.

There is a dilemma in the identity approach, and it has to do with reasonable accommodation: Today, employers are expected to accommodate reasonably. For example, a "no weapons" policy can be reasonably accommodated, the courts have ruled. It is important for our society to protect religious freedom. It is within this framework of "reasonable accommodation" that in 2007, Quebec's laws examined issues of cultural differences.

But what are the benefits of reasonable accommodation? Dr. Eisenberg believes it can create disadvantages for minorities. What are the problems with reasonable accommodation? She says the framework does well where minorities and mainstream peoples feel similarly on the issues. The more fundamental the way of doing things, the lesser opportunity for reasonable accommodation. Sometimes reasonable accommodation is expensive and causes major reform or undue hardship.

On the downside, Dr. Eisenberg believes religious accommodation can entrench the power of identity groups. "It stigmatizes minorities and sees them as different. But legal scholarship is optimistic that this can work."

In concluding remarks, she said there are some scholars who believe that there are greater challenges when fundamental religious practice or religious accommodation is made on the basis of identity politics and that our institutions should, therefore, discourage identity claiming. But she also believes it's unrealistic to ask institutions not to deal with these claims anymore. There is no reason to suppose these claims are going to go away soon.

Dr. Eisenberg claims democratic space is necessary, according to legal and political scholars. The hope is that this will motivate courts to advance Canada's human rights. In the real world, identity claiming cannot be divorced from the strategies of other forms of politics. "Accommodating other beliefs is easy, but accommodating religious practice is a problem," she says. "'Saturday is a holy day' is a belief. That's fine. 'I cannot work on Saturday' – that's religious practice."

THE RISK OF RADICALIZATION

Father Raymond J. de Souza, who delivered the keynote address at the 2011 Spiritual Diversity Conference hosted in Halifax presented his observations on the topic: How Can We Respond to the Challenges presented by Religious Diversity in Canada. He addressed five dimensions to the perspective: Here's an excerpt:

"First, religion has been a growing factor in global public life in the late 20th and early 21st century. This has an impact on Canadian public life as well, partly through immigration and partly through more assertive religious identity. Second, religious liberty is the first liberty and an essential public one, so any liberal democratic society has to make room for the religious in public life. Third, Canadian multiculturalism must take into account religious identity and practice, for culture at its heart is religious. Fourth, the diversity question is not about whether there is enough room for different religions, but whether there is room for religion at all. The battle as it were, is not between religions but between the aggressively secular and the religious. Fifth, the danger is this: the growth of secular fundamentalism in public life can be successful in marginalizing religious voices, but at the risk of radicalizing.

"We have seen this in some of the most secular nations in Europe. Their multicultural projects have been officially declared failures because large numbers of immigrants have declared themselves uninterested in becoming secular hedonists, and therefore built parallel societies in which radicalism has flourished."

Reverend de Souza was making the point that precisely by denying any role for religion in public life, it has been driven to the margins, where it has developed precisely the pathologies one expects to find at the margins. He concluded saying: "Our Canadian experience is not this. It's our challenge of diversity and remains our contribution toward a just and peaceful society."

COPING WITH RELIGIOUS DIVERSITY

Although the immigration portfolio has traditionally been, and still is, Ottawa's mandate, in recent years, most Canadian metropolitan centres have taken an interest in immigration because one recognizes the fact that diversity management is part of municipal administration.

"This is not surprising given the roles of people of immigrant origin in metropolitan populations. What is surprising is the reaction to religious diversity," observes

Annick Germain, Professor and Researcher at INRS, Canada.[9]

"In the Montreal area, where increasingly diversified immigration is commonplace, the establishment of places of worship associated with cultural minorities seems to have taken municipal officials by surprise both in the downtown core and in the suburbs."

She affirms that some officials have even declared a moratorium to give themselves time to review their zoning regulations or to seek the intervention of courts or the government. "As a result, in many municipalities, the construction of new places of worship is not automatically allowed and must follow an often complex and highly political process of special permits."

Germain's view is that the length of time people have been migrating to a community and the community's volume of immigration are often preconditions to build a place of worship. It is important to note that this new challenge of coping with religious diversity is a relatively new one since immigration did not begin to diversify - in terms of the numbers of non-Europeans - until well over a few decades ago.

---

[9] Annick Germain: "Religious Diversity: A Problem for Municipalities."

Montreal's religious landscape already includes more than just Catholic and Protestant churches. But the urban fabric of Montreal has always been marked by religious institutions. So what has changed?

"First, the volume of immigration has had an impact on the urban landscape: approximately 35 percent of the places of worship on Montreal Island are associated with specific immigrant or ethno religious groups," Germain says. "There has also been a rise in Eastern, non-Christian religions such as Islam, Sikhism and Buddhism. And with that, there has been an increase in churches associated with Reform Protestantism, which attracts both immigrants and native-born Canadians."

In terms of space, many small communities, have established worship centres in industrial parks and unused commercial zones, if not in the privacy of residences. The fact that so-called visible minorities frequent these places of worship obviously accentuates the phenomenon. In addition, these places of worship are no longer concentrated in inner cities: they can now be found in the suburbs and on the outskirts of the city.

Germain contends that because these worship centres are built away from the downtown core, they are no longer neighbourhood facilities, as parish churches were. "Since the communities are scattered throughout the metropolitan area and because land is scarce and expensive, places of worship increasingly operate regionally and, consequently, often have neighbours who do not share their religious conviction."

The pertinent question would be: why do so many municipal officials consider this explosion of places of worship to be a problem? Obviously, the principal issue is economics, Germain affirms. "In Quebec, places of worship are exempt from property and school taxes. This means that for municipalities, a place of worship translates into a loss of revenue."

This does not present a problem when land is not scarce. However, when the economy begins to grow, municipalities tend to give preference to a high-tech firm rather than to a Hindu temple as they develop their industrial parks. The municipalities are grappling with options to manage such complex issues and zoning indeed has its limits, beginning with classifying places of worship. Therefore, decisions cannot be based solely on regulations. "It is no coincidence that many issues surrounding the building of places of worship have created controversies and political compromises." Briefly, religious diversity, in the context of licencing worship centres, poses a challenge to municipalities.

How can education help? Education fosters tolerance and understanding. It holds in contempt race driven prejudice and dispels ignorance which is the foundation of race-driven hate.

CHAPTER IV

THE THREAT OF WAR

Despite the grave, bloody atrocity that World War II unleashed on the world between 1939 and 1945 in which some 60-85 million people perished, world leaders in the 21st century are, regardless, preoccupied with the nuclear button. In the last couple of decades, the world body has been coming together in organized summits to deter nuclear proliferation but the threat of nuclear warfare stares us in the face every time a nuclear weapon is tested or conflict and war break out and countries engage in sabre rattling.

I do not want to point fingers to aggressive political threats and tell the world what it already knows. Instead, I choose to present a case for what the world body can do to, at least, diminish the appetite for war.

R. J. Rummel, author of *Death by Government*, provides a provoking account of the democides committed specifically by four regimes, namely the former Soviet Union, China under Kai-shek, communist China and Nazi Germany.

In his preface to the book, he says: "The primary purpose was not to describe democide itself, but to determine its nature and test the theory that democracies are inherently nonviolent."[1]

The results, he affirms, decisively show that democracies commit less democide than totalitarian regimes do and that freedom and violence are inversely proportional. He then presents the doctrine of the Power Principle: power kills, absolute power kills absolutely.

That, I think, is a fair commentary on what drives nations to war. The Power Principle. That does not suggest, of course, that democracies are, necessarily, peace loving countries, though it does argue the fact that power is central to the threat of war. How do you deal with that? Nuclear war is a global catastrophic risk. The world has to wake up so as to stop a handful of powerful tyrants from setting the globe on fire.

The end of World War I must have brought a fresh breath of air to Europe and the world as it limped back from its state of shock to some normalcy. The resolve by a comity of nations to provide deterrents to war and the tools to perpetuate peace finally led to the formation of the League of Nations which, of course, was seemingly visionary at the time.

---

[1] R.J. Rummel, *Death by Government*, 1st edition (Jan. 1, 1997). Reproduced by permission of Taylor & Francis Group.

Let's examine briefly how the formation of the League of Nations; the work of its successor, the United Nations, its peacekeeping forces; and the North Atlantic Treaty Organization (NATO) have, in our time, got a handle on the job of keeping the world at peace.

Woodrow Wilson had an inspiring role in the creation of the League of Nations—the first worldwide intergovernmental organisation whose principal mission was to sustain world peace, after the Allied victory in World War 1 in November 1918. Wilson and the British and French leaders successfully advocated for its creation at the Paris Peace Conference, which was then incorporated into the Treaty of Versailles that he signed on 28 June 1919.[2]

The League's primary work stated in its Covenant spanned a slew of goals from the pre-emption of war, collective security and disarmament and the settling of international disputes through negotiation and arbitration.[3] The diplomatic philosophy behind the League represented a fundamental shift from the preceding

---

[2] "Treaty of Versailles" Archived from the original on 19 January 2010.

[3] "Covenant of the League of Nations". The Avalon Project. Archived from the original on 26 July 2011. Retrieved 30 August 2011.

hundred years. That was all well and good. But the League was deprived of the muscle to deter war – a noble vision mature beyond its time - and so it relied on its victorious First World War Allies: Britain, France, Italy and Japan to enforce its resolutions, keep to its economic sanctions, or provide an army when needed.

That was a commitment the Great Powers shirked, citing the fact that sanctions could hurt League members. Well, after some notable successes and some early failures in the 1920s, the League ultimately proved incapable of preventing aggression by the Axis powers in the 1930s, and the credibility of the organization was weakened by the fact that the United States never joined the League and the Soviet Union joined late and was soon expelled after invading Finland. Later, Germany withdrew from the League, as did Japan, Italy, Spain and others.[4]

The organization was finally dissolved after paving the way for the creation of the United Nations on October 24, 1945. How has the world changed since then?

---

[4] Ellis, Charles Howard (2003). *The Origin, Structure & Working of the League of Nations*. Lawbook Exchange Ltd., p. 169.

One notable consequence is that the five nation nuclear giants represented on the UN Security Council (UNSC) have, with maturity, eluded a war among themselves since World War II, although that has not stopped them from going to war with other UN member states. This might even suggest that a balance of power is in itself a nuclear deterrent, and that convoluted logic might provide a clue to why nations aspire to be nuclear armed. A case of the old adage holding true: you're damned if you do and you're damned if you don't.

Of course, there have been armed conflicts among nations outside the big-5 including the Indo-Pakistani War of 1971, the Iran–Iraq War (1980–1988), and the Gulf War of 1990–91. Three of the big five were involved in these conflicts. The other conflicts have been largely insurgencies.

The Arab Spring was a series of anti-government protests, uprisings, and armed rebellions that spread across much of the Arab world in the early 2010s. It began in response to corruption and economic stagnation and was first started in Tunisia.[5] The protests

---

[5] "Peddler's martyrdom launched Tunisia's revolution." *Reuters*. 19 Jan 2011. https://en.wikipedia.org/wiki/Arab_Spring#

then spread to Libya, Egypt, Yemen, Syria and Bahrain and four of the six rulers were booted out, imprisoned, deposed or killed.

The United Nations, apparently, lacked the mandate to intervene in ways that would halt the insurgencies and save lives. It has a mandate to prevent threats to peace, but as political commentators assert, the guiding principles of the United Nations sometimes serve as barriers to progress limiting strategic intervention. That limiting ability to operate comes from a complex interplay between the UN principles of self-determination and non-interference.

Consequently, on April 2016, Staffan de Mistura, the UN Syria envoy, told journalists after a meeting on Syria peace talks in Geneva, that 400,000 people had died in the Syrian war.[6]

Naturally, there have been calls for UN reform. On 21 September 2016, Saudi Crown Prince Mohammed bin Nayef bin Abdul Aziz Al-Saud told the General Assembly's annual general debate: "The United Nations needs urgent reform to confront the challenges now facing the world, from the Palestinian-Israel

---

[6] Syria death toll: UN envoy estimates 400,000 killed. *Al Jazeera*. Archived from the original on 24 April 2016. Retrieved 23 April 2016.

conflict and the bloody wars in Syria and Yemen to countering terrorism and tackling the refugee crisis."

He told the world body's General Assembly: "We are at a pivotal stage. We either join together in a collective effort to address the difficult challenges and disasters we are confronted with in the world or fail and in doing so history will not be on our side."[7]

The United Nations has been criticized for its policy, ideology, structure of representation, its inability to enforce rulings or act to de-escalate conflicts, as well as for the rampant antisemitism, appeasement, collusion, the promotion of globalism, thus subjugating national sovereignty and the abuse of power by nations influencing Assembly policy.[8] In 2004, Dore Gold, former Permanent Representative of Israel to the United Nations and author of the book *Tower of Babble: How the United Nations Has Fueled Global Chaos,* criticized what it called the organization's moral relativism in the face of (and occasional support of) genocide and terrorism.[9]

It has been criticized for being an exclusive nuclear club with five nuclear powers sitting on the United

---

[7] UN News.

[8] wikipedia.org/wiki.criticism_of_the_United_Nations

[9] Ibid. Gold, pp. 216–217.

Nations Security Council board. A consequence of that structure is that a veto from any of the permanent members can halt the passing of a UN resolution. One country's objection, rather than the opinions of a majority of nations, may cripple any possible UN armed or diplomatic response to a crisis.

The world body has been criticized, as well, for its failure in the handling of Sri Lanka's civil war, the 100-day massacre in the Rwanda crisis and the positions it has taken in support of national liberation movements including the Palestinian cause.[10]

UN Peacekeeping was created in 1948 at the end of World War II and as of 30 June 2019, there were 100,411 people serving in UN peacekeeping operations. The organization operates with a budget of $6.7 billion.[11]

It was created to partner with countries torn by conflict and to create the conditions for lasting peace. Keep in mind, peacekeepers remain members of their respective armed forces and do not constitute an independent "UN army." They are deployed—often unarmed—to areas where warring parties express a need

---

[10] Ibid.

[11] "Data/United Nations Peacekeeping" UN, 30 June 2019.

for a neutral party to observe the peace process. UN peacekeeping forces cannot stop a war. So let's move on. What's the other neutral option?

The North Atlantic Treaty Organization (NATO), which is an intergovernmental military alliance among 28 European and two North American countries was set up in the aftermath of World War II, in 1949.[12] It constitutes a system of collective security and independent member states agree to mutual defense in response to an attack by an external party.

NATO, unlike the UN peacekeeping forces, is a military organization. But it's a European alliance that provides only member states a system of collective security. So when after the September 11 attacks on the Twin Towers in New York, President George W. Bush declared a war on the Taliban, NATO could engage in the war effort only after invoking Article 5 of its Charter which states that an attack on any member shall be considered to be an attack on all. The invocation was confirmed on 4 October 2001, and NATO agreed to take command of the International Security Assistance

---

[12]   "What   is   NATO?". *NATO   -   Homepage.* Archived from the original on 28 February 2022. Retrieved 3 March 2022.

Force (ISAF), which included troops from 42 countries.[13]

On similar grounds, NATO has gotten involved, as well, in other operations across the world.

NATO, indeed, is a military organization and has ended wars. But it's an organization with security interests limited to Europe and North America. How do we keep the peace elsewhere in the world? What tools does the world body have to stop the Russia-Ukraine war?

So the question on everyone's mind now is just how is Ukraine alone going to fight this war with Russia ? It's not yet a member of NATO, and the organization will not get involved unless Russia encroaches its territory. The US and European countries too will not want to intervene so as to abide by the sovereignty principle and the principle of non-interference in the affairs of nations. The US President has, of course, asked Congress to approve $33 billion in aid to Ukraine.

What's the way out? How do we present a safer world to our grandkids?

---

[13]   Münch, Philipp (2021). "Creating common sense:Getting NATO to Afghanistan".*Journal of Transatlantic Studies*. 19 (2): 138–166. January 2013. https://en.wikipedia.org/wiki/NATO

Stop and think for a moment of the state of our world. Eight sovereign states have publicly announced successful detonation of nuclear weapons. Of them, five aforementioned nations represented on the UN Security Council are considered to be nuclear-weapon states (NWS) under the terms of the Treaty on the Non-Proliferation of Nuclear Weapons (NPT).

Since the NPT entered into force in 1970, three other states that were not parties to the Treaty have conducted nuclear tests, namely India, Pakistan and North Korea. Isn't that an urgent enough reason for the world body to get together and seriously examine the risks and then map out a plan to take a step back and give peace a chance?

What are the options? Is a reformed and re-structured United Nations a pragmatic option? Do we need a world army – with the muscle to deter and stop a war, structured on the lines of NATO, that will serve the world body, stepping in to intervene when any one of the world's 195 nations is threatened?

I really don't know. But what I do know is: first, that you cannot drive away darkness with darkness; light can do that and, second, that the world body can come together and come up with a vision to safeguard the human race in the foreseeable future.

I can imagine two scenarios: First, in the short term, perhaps one must work on revamping the United Nations, broadening its control centre to include other influential nations on the Security Council, defining veto by a majority vote and giving the organization – the world body - the power to respond pragmatically to conflict.

Second, the long term view of a world free of war should guide us along a path that creates a non-violent society. In much the same way as we must prepare the social climate in which the seed of economic development can germinate—in other words a climate that fosters literate societies, that most powerful tool to end poverty— we must likewise prepare the climate for a peaceable world society in which war will be defined as a dirty word and will be met with contempt.

I am a pacifist and do not believe that war is the path to peace. If this must be achieved, we must go back to the drawing board. If peace can be achieved by understanding, its meaning must penetrate the minds of our kids.

How do you do that? Let's start with our kids: introduce them to books not to toy guns; to sport, not to violence on television screens. Let's reform our education curricula—nudge our kids to abhor violence— make it a household word in our schools. Preach peace in our classrooms. We need to create a society that cherishes humanity and thinks of violence as an abomination.

The task of taking on this life-changing dream is a challenge for UNESCO – the organization that has been entrusted with the world's aspirations in education, science and culture.

Go on. "Do not follow where the path may lead. Go instead where there is no path and leave a trail," said Ralph Waldo Emerson. "You see things; and you say, 'Why?' But I dream things that never were; and I say, 'Why not?'" said George Bernard Shaw.

In just the same way as the widespread development of Japanese education after World War II served to shape the creation of a highly educated workforce that was key to Japan's remarkable economic resurgence, grassroots education built around the appreciation of a non-violent society can transform man's aspirations and the desire to inhabit a world that eschews violence and embraces peace.

Indoctrination! Give peace a chance! Create a social climate in which despots do not germinate—a climate in which moral character shines and thrives and a generation of educated men and women preach compassion and peace. It would take a decade or two to taste the first fruits of this garden of Eden. But in the life of nations, a decade is like an evening gone.

CHAPTER V

NATIONAL MORALITY

Why would I be talking about morality in a book that's seeking to lay out new challenges in the life of nations? You got it! The reformation of the morality of nations can be as challenging as the task of eliminating poverty in the developing world, confronting the new realities of a rapidly emerging migration movement or holding back the instinct for war.

It has long been acknowledged that citizens of a state have, in almost all cases, definite traits of national character which bring them together as one people bonded by a set of spiritual beliefs, custom, traditions and linguistic commonality. It is this commonality of national character that sets one nation apart from another, promoting a sense of nationhood. The conversation, yet, has to begin with a defining note on what is morality?

Simply stated, it's conformity to ideals of right human conduct. In the normative sense, "morality" refers to a code of conduct that would be accepted by anyone who meets the intellectual and volitional conditions, almost always including the condition of being rational.[1]

So what has morality got to do with state governance? Isn't that a private matter to which an individual conscience bows? Not quite. It would be fair to suggest that if an individual's conscience does actually bow to a moral law, it would seem consequential that the state would seek for itself a moral code. It can be argued that since the state is nothing but the people it represents, the state ought to be moral as the individual is moral.

Erudite philosophers through the ages in history have shone a light on the desirability of a sterling national morality that is shaped by the sacred laws presented by the Creator. "In God We Trust" is the official motto of the United States of America and was adopted by the U.S. Congress in 1956, replacing *E pluribus unum*, which had been the de facto motto since the initial 1776 design of the Great Seal of the United States.[2]

---

[1] Standard Encyclopedia of Philosophy: The Definition of Morality. https://plato.stanford.edu/entries/morality-definition

[2] Bittker, Boris; Idleman, Scott; Ravitch, Frank (2015). *Religion and the State in American Law*. Cambridge University Press. p. 136. Archived from the original on 2021-04-22.

What we have come to realize over the centuries is that morality can be central to the spirit of nations. That is because nations have chosen to be theocracies, and we see this in Europe, in the Middle East and South East Asia as well. Going back to biblical history, we are told that Sodom and Gomorrah—the two legendary biblical cities—were destroyed by God for their licentiousness and their story parallels the Genesis flood narrative. (Genesis 19:1-28)

The state, which is a political institution, defines its national character by a set of beliefs, customs and tradition, a spirituality, whether secular or not, its respect of human rights and a foreign policy that reflects the nation's desire to be a part of the global society. Seen in the light of that definition, the state adheres to a broad principle of morality which it confers on its people and expects from them adherence to that principle. A state may choose liberalism or may choose conservatism—that generally reflects the character and aspirations of its people. So what you see in some states of the Muslim and Arab world is that alcohol is regulated or prohibited. In some Christian nations, perhaps abortion is not legalised. In Hindu societies, a conservative dress code is respected and the consumption of beef is scorned and banned. These are morality principles that a state lays down.

W.R. Sorley, a Scottish philosopher (1855-1935) writing in the *International Journal of Ethics* on "The Morality of Nations" observes: "The individual has duties to the state and perhaps rights against it in turn; while the state, within certain limits, controls the action of the individual: educating him perhaps, laying down laws for his social and industrial behavior, and compelling him to contribute of his property, and even to sacrifice his liberty of action and risk his life, in defence of her integrity and the objects which she holds worthy of a nation's endeavor."[3]

But apparently, the matter is contentious. The world's secular societies have long held the view that morality is driven by the natural order of human consciousness. It's commonly assumed that people act in ways that are dictated by a moral obligation; that morality commits us to that social consciousness; that society does not have to rely on a moral lawgiver; the world can be moral without God. How true is this?

Let's look at the morality of European society up until the Edict of Milan in 313 AD. Europe was pagan

---

[3] "The Morality of Nations" by W.R. Sorley https://www.journals.uchicago.edu/doi/pdf/10.1086/intej ethi.1.4.2375489

in its morality and its emperors actually turned a blind eye to the morally shameful practice of infanticide.

Slavery, which prevailed long before Jesus' time, was a flourishing trade and women were subjugated – anti-Samaritan prejudices actually forbade respectable men from speaking to Samaritan women in public.

In a morally bankrupt milieu such as this, Jesus of Nazareth brought about a wind of change that swept across the region. His Sermon on the Mount introduced a new spiritual morality in the West that was to survive the next two millennia and beyond.

When in 313 AD, Emperor Constantine I rolled out the Edict of Milan, the Roman society in Europe fell apart and its old gods perished in the temples. Christianity seized that moment and changed the moral ethos of nations. The Philemon and Galatian scriptural passages declared: "There is neither Jew nor Greek, there is neither slave nor free person, there is not male and female; for you are all one in Christ Jesus." (Galatians 3:28 NAB) That declaration in scripture laid the foundation for the abolition of slavery for the future.

Cambridge philosopher Elizabeth Anscombe argued way back in 1958 that the concept of moral obligation in Western philosophy has its roots in Christianity, which perceives of ethics and morality in terms of laws given by God. Anscombe was absolutely right.

The claim that societal construct is the compelling force driving moral obligation is easily dismissed and cannot stand as the truth. Think of the brutalities of the two world wars and the evil that unfolds on our streets everyday: the suicide bombings and the mass killing of innocent people: a car rams into crowds during white supremacist marches in Charlottesville in the United States; a van ploughs into pedestrians on Westminster Bridge in London. Across the world, we see autocratic or tyrannical regimes pushing forth an amoral agenda, carried out by civil servants who see obedience to these amoral dictates as societal obligations. A culture of deceit sweeps across the political ethos of many nations.

No. I think the moral law comes from the Creator alone and not from social consciousness.

Moral decline may have been gradual through the centuries, but in our time in the 21st century, the nature of its decline is scary. In recent decades, the decline perhaps took root during the dark days of the post-World War II depression which ignited a bouncing back frenzy to a consuming world inspired by what was being described as the emerging culture of the 1960s.

That movement brought about the liberation of self and the casting off of restraint. Now, most young teenagers today are dreaming of piling up millions. A soccer star might rank first among some of their heroes and God might just be an idea. The grain of moral values has eroded to a point that the recent American elections which ejected Donald Trump out of the White House put "character and decency" on the top rung of the Presidential morality ladder.

Our youth are taught to navigate the waters of life through power, wealth and fame. The trending notion is that man is master of his fate and captain of his soul. It's a laughing matter to me. Can I really be made to believe that I am master of my fate when, in fact, I am in control of nothing? Words of a song are ringing in my ears at this time: "How can you stop the rain from falling down? How can you stop the sun from shining?"[4] And for goodness sake, can I put an end to death?

The drift to godlessness and the plunge into hedonism was gradual as well. Our societies seek gratification from alcohol and drug abuse, wild parties, sensual pleasures, violence and so forth. The tradition of moral uprightness has gradually shifted with people embracing a culture of self-emancipation, a freedom-seeking culture that casts out all restraint or controls on

---

[4] Song by the Bee Gees: "How can you mend a broken heart?"

societal behavior, introducing a culture of irreverence that ignores moral righteousness.

In a book I dedicated to my seven grandkids last Christmas I wrote: "Remember: only dead fish swim with the tide. It is therefore important for you to discern with maturity what you think is right and wrong. Collectively, smoking, alcohol abuse and illicit drug use kills 11.8 million people each year."[5]

The abuse of alcohol, gambling and promiscuity can destroy young lives. The mistakes one makes today could worry us for a long, long time. It's common knowledge that some of the rich and famous who have got to the top rungs in politics or corporate ladders, have fallen to disgrace and many of them languish in jail for the wrongs they did in their youth. Unbridled emancipation, the casting out of restraint, and irreverence in one's conduct are apparently precursors to teenage pregnancies, violence at home and other amoral behaviours.

The 21st century has seen crime shift from the streets to online platforms. As a result, crime may have just migrated in a higher proportion to the online sphere. Halifax Police Chief Jean-Michel Blais told me that a study out of Britain showed that eighty percent of

---

[5] https://ourworldindata.org/drug-use

people had been victimized online. The laptop can very easily be transformed into an evil weapon troubling young minds with pornography. The bitcoin currency has made seeking ransom a cakewalk. At the state level, we see deceit. We take pro-life positions on abortion, but we uphold capital punishment. We look upon tribal warfare with scorn, but we need guns to defend ourselves. That's life in the 21st century.

The drift to godlessness in early history may have been driven by man's licentious behaviour and the soul's incapacity to conceive of an invisible Creator. It was simpler, at the time, to worship the golden calf and adorn it in defiance. But in the 21st century although godlessness is driven by the same factors, it is perpetuated by a growing acceptance of the notion that God is a delusion and which is why morality does not matter. So, it's timely to quickly review the notions ordinary secularists present to discredit God.

Science, we are told, offers the view that creation occurred at a single moment with the Big Bang —about 14 billion years ago—when a ball of powerful energy exploded. The narrative then goes on to say that after the initial expansion, the universe cooled sufficiently to allow the formation of subatomic particles and later simple atoms causing giant clouds of these primordial elements—mostly hydrogen and helium— to coalesce through gravity in halos of dark matter, to eventually form the stars and galaxies, the descendants of which are visible today.[6]

It's not surprising that the scientific world is divided on the truth of this story. The British astronomer, Sir Fred Hoyle, was one among them who flagrantly rejected the Big Bang theory. So be it!

Going back in history, Charles Darwin first aroused great euphoria in the world of science with his book *On The Origin of Species*. The expectation was that the question about how life began would soon be resolved. But that was not to be. My sense is that most of those who have read Darwin's first editions of "Origin" are likely unaware of the fact that in his sixth edition of the book, he spoke of life taking its form from the breath of the Creator. He wrote, "Therefore I should infer from analogy that probably all organic beings which have ever lived on this earth have descended from one primordial form into which life was first breathed by the Creator."[7]

---

[6] Peebles P.J.E.; Ratra Bharat, 22 April 2003. "The cosmological constant and dark energy". Reviews of Modern Physics 75 (2) 559-606.

[7] Darwin, Charles, *On the Origin of Species*, The Project Gutenberg eBook, Chapter X1V: Recapitulation and Conclusion, final paragraph, Sixth edition.

You see, Darwin never really spoke of origins. He spoke about the evolution of life.

The 1953, Miller-Urey experiment with amino acids was seeking to determine, if by serendipity, chemicals mixing in an organized way somewhere in an ocean could actually join together to form proteins and subsequently combine into symbiotic relationships. That was a non-starter.

The scientist Gerald Schroeder who wrote the book *The Hidden Face of God*, affirms that "we can predict all elements used in life, but there is no indication that we can predict amino acids joining together in chains of thousands of units to form proteins and then proteins combining into symbiotic relationships we refer to as life." He goes on to say: "The emergence of the specialized complexity of life, even in its most simplest forms, remains a bewildering mystery."[8]

A bewildering mystery, indeed! Try this out: On a starry night, gaze at the stars and wonder! Then pause and ponder over the physical constants in their Goldilocks zones which make the planet hospitable to life; marvel at the colors of the rainbow, the breaking dawn, the birthing of a child and believe!

---

[8] Schroeder, L. Gerald, *The Hidden Face of God*, Simon & Schuster, p. 58. Reprinted with permission.

The mystics will tell you that you do not have to see in order to believe. Instead believe, so that you may see! The Christian disciple Thomas had refused to believe the narrative of the resurrection of Jesus until he put his hand in His side. Jesus then said to him: "Thomas, because thou hast seen Me, thou hast believed. Blessed are they that have not seen and yet have believed." (John 20:29)

If science were to prove God, who would want to pray or worship such a God? We do not worship the Pythagorean Theorem, do we? So, close your eyes and open your hearts and you will find God in there! Morality does matter.

The question that comes up in this morality discourse is this: How does moral decline affect national life and economic progress?

It is a foregone conclusion now that globalisation and economic integration is a salient feature of the modern world. Political tensions may considerably hinder all aspects of economic integration. The tussle between western powers and the rest of the world has been to seek common ground in state partnerships where government policy and operations are inspired by democratic traditions and on their moral position especially on issues connected with human rights. That these criteria for state partnerships are not always applied across the board is not for me to comment. It is a fact of life, nonetheless, that the warming and cooling of political ties between countries is accompanied by expansion and contraction of their trade operations. State policy, if not morally respectable, will obviously hinder healthy political ties between nations of the world.

TIME FOR A NEW AWAKENING?

We need to challenge ourselves with those grave questions: Where have I come from? Why am I here? Where am I going? How can we end this passage of life without a perspective on the purpose of it all? When one comes to that point in the search for the truth, a new morality evolves.

Nations, I believe, can foster morality, secular though it may be, and transform societies to become responsive to the collective needs of their countrymen, promoting truth and honest conduct, a respect for human rights and social justice and a collective acceptance of the golden rule taught by all of the world's religious traditions, which is to do unto others that which you would like others do unto you.

The founder of the Jesuit Brotherhood, St Ignatius Loyola, famously declared in his time: "Give me a child till he is seven years old, and I will show you the man."

The Jesuits, who manage some of the best schools across the world, are famously known to focus on the young, when the formation of neural networks, according to reports, are governed by emotion and so mould a child's behaviour as they launch out into adult life.

Moral conduct must be the cornerstone of education in our schools so that we begin to alter the way the human race connects with one another at a tender age. The future can grow and be promising if man has grasped the secret to making peace with another. Morality builds character and shapes the behavior of the human being. He or she embraces life with compassion, tolerance, welcomes into the world the poor, the atheist, another point of view. He or she brings light to drive away the darkness, hope in the midst of despair, compassion where there is hate and reason where insanity festers.

If we are looking to transform our world and create societies with character, we must start at the drawing board and mold our citizens in their early schooling tenures. Change cannot come overnight.

In recognition of the notion that peace requires the involvement of peoples of all faiths, the Baha'i International Community affirms that it is becoming increasingly clear that passage to the culminating stage in the millennia-long process of the organization of the planet as one home for the entire human family cannot be accomplished in a spiritual vacuum.

The Baha'i scriptures proclaim:

"Religion is the source of illumination, the cause of development and the animating impulse of all human advancement and has been the basis of all civilization and progress in the history of mankind. It is the source of meaning and hope for the vast majority of the planet's inhabitants and has a limitless power to inspire sacrifice, change and long-term commitment in its followers. It is, therefore, inconceivable that a peaceful and prosperous global society—a society which nourishes a spectacular diversity of cultures and nations—can be established and sustained without directly and substantively involving the world's great religions in its design and support."[9]

---

[9] Extract from a presentation by Gordon Naylor of the National Spiritual Assembly of the Bahá'is of Canada, delivered at the 2011 Spiritual Diversity Conference in Halifax.

The state of our world today calls for multifaith literacy to be taught in our schools. We cannot embrace our fellow citizens if we're ignorant of their culture and religion. The economies we have today and the world order we have designed, have been shaped by the education that our schools presented to us some decades ago. But then, of course, you reap as you sow. If our history books glorify war, we create a society that glorifies war. By the same token, if our history books glorify peacemakers, we create a society that glorifies peace. If school curriculums ignore the development of a pluralist society, our kids will turn to newcomers with suspicion and some with hate. If that's multiplied many times over, it's enough ammunition to let hate fester and explode on our streets.

Get this right: multiculturalism is not going to leave Western shores anytime in the future. Instead, it's going to be the mainstay if our economies have to grow. That being said, shouldn't our school curriculums introduce multifaith literacy programs to empower students for positive social change?

Syed Adnan, a Professor of Religion at Saint Mary's University in Halifax told me some time ago: Multifaith literacy is more than really grasping the facts about other traditions. Multifaith literacy cannot be merely con-strued as communicating concepts across faiths, but rather should lead us to a deep understanding of the other.

In the first decade of this century prior to and after the bombing of the twin towers in New York, violence broke out in a way that it upended the state of the world. Al Qaida chief Osama Bin Laden, sought to put an end to US hegemony and what was perceived as Christian dominance of the West and so ordered the bombing of the Twin Towers. That dreaded cataclysm almost divided the world into two and ignited two wars, one looking for Bin Laden in the caves of Afghanistan and the other looking to topple Saddam Hussein who was suspected of producing weapons of mass destruction.

Muslim scholars in the aftermath of 9/11 kicked off a rigorous campaign of damage control, inviting groups from non-Muslim societies to seminars and presentations in order to familiarise them with the teachings of the Koran. That was surely welcome. In time, the Western world was ready to concede that a minority group of fundamentalists were waging this war in God's name and that their actions were nowhere reflected in the Muslim Holy Book.

Syed Mustaffa al Qazwini in his presentation to delegates at the 2016 Spiritual Diversity Conference in the city of Halifax declared: "Islam respects and accepts differences and calls for embracing commonalities. The

Golden Rule is found in every defined religion. In Arabic, you find this in the words of the Prophet. He says: "Love and wish for your brethren which you love and wish for yourself and dislike for him and her what you dislike for yourself."

EPILOGUE

A nuclear war will bring the world to its knees and civilization will be a faint idea for those who inherit the earth. So that's not the world we want to leave for our grandkids. History will hold us up in contempt. We must brace for change. The scourge of poverty, race, religion and the threat of war have troubled our world for centuries, shedding blood, sweat and tears along the expanse of time. War is ugly and its progenitors belong outside the bounds of civilization.

So, what this book has sought to do is bring brilliant minds to the table to examine the nature of whatever enslaves us to a future that's doomed and to probably review the options at hand that can bring about change even at the cost of going back to the drawing board to dream up new ways of making life truly civilized and subsequently sustainable.

In my mind, I can point to only education as the key to creating an ideal world. Iraqi booksellers, who leave their books out in the open in the night have a saying: "Our readers do not steal and thieves cannot read." What this says to me is: "If we create readers, we also get rid of thieves." We can create elite societies and peaceable communities by introducing moral conduct into the curricula of school education.

A well-rounded education is key to the challenge of change. Academic literacy eliminates poverty by engaging societies in economic development. It moderates migration and the movement of people outside their national borders because in literate societies, the jobs are in the home country. It scorns race-driven prejudice and dispels ignorance which is the foundation of race-driven hate. Likewise, moral literacy creates a society that abhors violence and the scourge of war and creates the climate in which nations are transformed and driven to spawn and engender peaceable generations. Education fosters national morality.

If morality is made the cornerstone of the education process from the cradle upwards across the world, education will shape moral character and may just be central to resolving some of the world's chronic problems, including troubles with poverty, migration worries, race and religion, the threat of war and national morality.

Education is not merely an economic development agent but a character builder, a morality progenitor, a virtue-driven engine, a peace broker, a literary agent—a tool that can end poverty, lower the unbridled growth of populations, instill abhorrence for violence and someday stop war.

ACKNOWLEDGMENTS

In 1997, after gleaning through extensive research, I came to the conclusion that poverty is not so much a consequence of low natural resources or bad economic management as it is of alarmingly low literacy levels in some parts of our world. So I set about writing the book *Can the Poor Inherit the Earth* in which I declared that there is strong concomitance between poverty and literacy. A spike in literacy, forces a proportionate drop in poverty. COMMACT, a grassroots organization, now headquartered in Australia, asked for a manuscript and went right ahead and published the book.

Now early this year, when I was clearing out the dust on my bookshelf, I ran my fingers through this book again and it occurred to me, after a brief read, that in the two decades since writing the book *Can the Poor Inherit the Earth*, my deductions founded on the principle of the concomitance of literacy and poverty were absolutely true. The spike in literacy in China and India, for example, had resulted in a proportionate drop in poverty.

Later in contemplation, I was drawn to envision another fact: that strategic education designed to build moral character and abhor violence among other things, may just be central to resolving some of the world's chronic problems, including troubles with migration, race and religion, the threat of war and national morality.

So I did a word sketch of this book *Global Healing* and rushed it to Dr. Sebastian Mahfood, OP, the publisher of En Route Books and Media in the United States. He got back to me the same day, saying: "Wonderful, Robin! Why don't you send me the book and I will send you a contract." I am grateful to Dr. Mahfood. This book would not have been in your hands but for his insightful vision.

I also acknowledge with gratitude, the many publishing houses, universities, data banks, UN organizations and other research organizations, who graciously granted me gratis permissions to reprint quotes from their copyrighted material under the fair use provisions of the copyright law.

I am grateful to the Honorary Editors Stephen Cunningham and Aaron Arthur who pored over the book and made keenly perceptive observations.

Finally, this book would not have been possible without my patient wife, Teresa, who gleaned through the pages of this book and presented me with some important insights.

* 9 7 8 1 9 5 6 7 1 5 5 5 2 *